Legacy of Grace

IT IS FINISHED
IT IS COMPLETE
IT IS ETERNAL

By Gary Pippins

Carwayne Publishing

THE LEGACY OF GRACE
© 2013 by Gary Pippins

All scripture quotations unless otherwise indicated, are taken from the International Standard Version of the Bible, ®Copyright 1966-2001, by ISV Foundation, used by permission, all rights reserved internationally.

All Greek and Hebrew definitions of English words unless otherwise indicated, are taken from The Strong Exhaustive Concordance of the Bible, ® Copyright ©1995, by Thomas Nelson, Inc. used by permission, all rights reserved.

Please note that the author chooses to change particular punctuations or words in the Scriptures for grammatical reasons. The author also chooses to capitalize specific pronouns in Scripture that refer to the Father, Son, and Holy Spirit; this may differ from some Bible publishers' styles. The author has added Scripture quotations with emphasis as noted.

ISBN-13: 978-0989371629 (Carwayne)
ISBN-10: 098937162X

Gary R. Pippins
kingdommotivations.com
For speaking engagements please contact at:
E-mail: garypippins@yahoo.com.

CARWAYNE
PUBLISHING
www.carwayne.com

Unto Us

Unto us a gift was given
Unto us grace was born
Unto us our sins forgiven
Unto us to be no more

Unto us our right position
Unto us as was before
Unto us none forbidden
Unto us an open door

Unto us is life eternal
Unto us for evermore
Unto us grace is granted
Unto us God's mercy swore

Gary R. Pippins

Moses gave the law, but grace and truth came through Jesus Christ *(John 1:17)*.

Contents

Chapter	1	Called and Chosen	7
Chapter	2	Transforming Grace	17
Chapter	3	The Gospel, What Is It?	21
Chapter	4	Starting Point of Grace	35
Chapter	5	Do We Need Grace?	49
Chapter	6	Repentance Brings Grace	63
Chapter	7	Abraham; Grace by Faith	73
Chapter	8	Dead to sin, Alive to Grace	83
Chapter	9	The Need for Grace	93
Chapter	10	Falling from Grace	107

To the front of the cross was the Law of sin and death. The sting of death is sin, and the power of sin is the law. (*One Corinthians 15:56*)

Behind the cross is the Law of God's grace by Faith. Through Christ the law of the Spirit sets us free from the Law of sin and death. (*Romans 8:2*)

Chapter One

Called and Chosen

Many sources agree Paul was born around the year five A.D. and executed in Rome in or about the year A.D. 65. Paul lived a very interesting short 60 years.

I believe if Paul were here and spoke to us today, he would proclaim the exact message he taught both Jews and Gentiles of his age, expressing the identical impassioned excitement. I believe this is what he would say to us on the subject of our Lord's legacy to all humanity.

"I Paul a servant of Jesus Christ was called to be an apostle and placed independently for the gospel of God Himself. It has been a great struggle, needless to say, to continue as a servant of Jesus Christ, mind and body, whom Christ Himself, by the authority of His Father God, set me apart in ministry.

I was an Apostle, a spiritual builder of many churches, a direct teacher of His good news concerning His grace throughout the world. I have witnessed, first hand, many miraculous signs and wonders. I am so humbled for His glorious goodness, and much undeserved favor.

Often referred to as the Apostle Paul or Saint Paul, I was born Saul of Tarsus, in south-Central Turkey. Although born in Tarsus, known for its intellectual environment, I was educated in Jerusalem. I am the son of a Pharisee, whom also is a son of a Pharisee, of the tribe of Benjamin. As a Pharisee myself, I speak proudly as a Hebrew of the Hebrews and fluent in the Laws of Moses as taught by the great Gamaliel, an Israelite. I am a leading authority to the Sanhedrin court.

Some say, I was the most influential servant of my day, manipulating the thinking of many unbelieving Jews as well as the Gentiles. God's plan for man is through a conversion to the only true Savior of the world, Jesus, who is the Christ. Many say, through my ministry, I helped turn a religious world back to its spiritual roots.

As a modest servant of Jesus Christ, I am truly thankful for His undeserved favor, which constantly sustains me and proves sufficient in all my journeys. Unfortunately, I have not always been the willing submissive follower of my Lord, for there were times, in which I greatly regret; I was forcefully persecuting His Church.

Persecuting God's Church

As a young man, and I say this not to boast, but as a testimonial of God's free grace, I stood by watching as a faithful follower of my Lord was stoned to his death. Stephan I believe was his name, and I stood guarding the coats of those performing his sentence of death. I can still envision that horrific act as he was stoned; not one time did he deny his faith! Even as he breathed his last breath, he cried out asking God to forgive them. His words still linger in the corridors of my mind. He said they didn't understand what they are doing.

Some say I was a demanding student of Gamaliel completely in line with Judaism while others saw a complaisant man in the middle of two extremes; one, a literal Ritual Law and on the other hand, God's gift of loving favor. A controversy between these two always was present; the act of ritual circumcision, awarding favor for personal good deeds performed, or a simple faith, awarding God's favor through the shed blood of Jesus the Christ.

Contrary to my own plan, religious ideologies accelerated the separation of His Gospel, the messianic sect of Christians from its traditional roots. Our faith in Christ alone is the decisive factor in receiving forgiveness for sin. Jewish people as well as Gentiles, men or women, young and old, you are equal before God, thus making any division a division of the mind only.

I proclaimed the doctrine of justification before God without any need of ritual circumcision. There was no longer the need of special dietary restrictions or observance of Mosaic Law to acquire favor from our Lord. The only positive value to the law towards humanity is to guide their moral character. Personal works are not a prerequisite to God's New Covenant blessing any longer, but seen only as a witness unto salvation.

The favor of God through faith in Jesus' shed blood is our true identity. The New Testament believer is justified by faith alone and not of works. Grace is the badge of courage, God's undeserved favor to all who follow in obedience to Christ, and we should wear it proudly, but also humbly.

Bond Servants

If you were a poor Hebrew boy, in my time, and found committing a theft, it was very possible you could be sold into slavery to clear your obligation to society. You would serve a task master six years, and then allowed your freedom, having justified your debt; all obligations of the law canceled. At the end of your sentence, if you were unmarried, you would leave as a single man. If you were married, your wife and children could leave with you. If you were single at the time of sentencing, your Master could allow you a wife, and if she had borne your children, they would belong and stay with the Master. If you, as his slave, would choose not to leave, you could as a bond slave stay and continue service. You would serve of your freewill to that Master's household.

Your Master would bring you to the door to his dwelling, for all to see. Using a puncturing tool, then pin your right ear to his doorpost, symbolizing; you are bonded as one, to that particular house. This showing, out of your devotion to the Master, you will serve his household voluntarily.

An oval ring would be then placed in the right-side ear lobe, signifying a right positioned bondservant. At that moment in time, you would become a willing slave until death. The ring being placed in the right ear symbolizes a precise position of true standing with the owner's household; now in absolute agreement, you will perform the desires of your master.

As with the bond slave, you were also purchased and your debt paid. Sin's ledger against all humanity was balanced; judgment was brought before the Supreme Court Justice of heaven. The debt inherited from Adam's rebellious act in the garden was canceled! Christ paid our debt, a debt; He did not owe a debt we could not pay. All past, present, and future sin was wiped away by His blood! Nothing can or will change that fact; this is why, why; His grace is so amazing! It's not only your debt that was paid, but of all of humanity; whosoever will come to Christ, will be ransomed and set free!

Any contradiction to this phenomenal gift of grace comes merely from a self-righteous mindset. We as believer's thinking, our personal mistakes are much greater than Christ's purest cleansing blood. Some may think; His blood is only able to wash some sin away, but the time-hardened sins; we need to help God clean. After all, one might think, we must do something to earn our way into heaven!

Now, stop, just take the time to think, wasn't this type of self-righteous mind-set, the very reason Jesus gave Himself as the ransom for your sin in the first place? Stop trying to live by the same rules Christ came to deliver you from; this is spiritually offensive to God. My fellow citizens of heaven, God did not send Jesus to earth to make bad men good, but He came to give a lively hope to all un-righteous souls doomed by Adam's rebellion; His legacy of grace is our only justification.

Jesus came to disclose the world's true godless nature and resurrect a spiritually dead world back into fellowship. Consider the prodigal son, the son was separated from any relationship (dead), but was restored (came back to fellowship); He was away from safety (lost, hidden by rebellion), but returned (found) (*Luke 15:2*). God's grace is free to everyone, but only given to those who believe and accept! It is this free grace, God's unmerited favor, which delivered you from His judgment. This salvation is not of human action; it didn't come through your personal efforts, but through the endowment of God, the fulfillment of the law, serving justice. Christ became "you're personal" justice; Salvation is not natural, but supernatural! No one can boast of any personal glory for Christ Himself became "you're personal" justice!

The regulatory law could only allow man to connect with God through acts of self-worth. Our New Covenant connection is through Christ's blood. Once for all, we are separate from any involvement except for the trust in His Word. Only through His cleansing blood can all become righteous enough to come boldly before Him.

The only human participation needed in God's plan of redemption is your acceptance through faith in His New Covenant. Think about this: if humanity had any part in this redemptive work, it would have been earthly, unclean and useless.

Grace Supersedes

I have never thought myself as being compared to those who are, as some refer, super-apostles. I have always made it clear, to all in every possible way, though I may be untrained in public speaking; I am well versed in the knowledge of God's law.

I became all things to all people, in order to win them to the cause of Christ. In some ways, I was a far better servant than many! If you were Hebrew, an Israelite, or a descendant of Abraham's children, sow was I, and if you were Christ's servant, so was I. I was involved in many great efforts, far more imprisonments, countless beatings, and looked death in the face more than once. In fact, I recall, being five times whipped upon my back; thirty-nine lash each! Three times I was beaten with a stick! Three times shipwrecked! One of those times I remember drifting in the sea for a whole day and a night!

Numerous journeys were made involving dangers from rivers, dangers from robbers, dangers from the Gentiles! There were dangers in the cities, dangers in the open country, dangers at sea and dangers from even those acting as close friends! I spent many sleepless nights in hunger and thirst outside my regular periods of fasting! I lived through the desert heat and cold, both clothed and naked. Let me tell you, I have had my share of tests and trials, which makes me worthy to proclaim His wonderful delivering grace. Once I too was attacked with stones and left for dead! Whether I was dead or alive, I don't know, only God knows! I was taken up into Paradise and heard things that can't be expressed in human words, things that any other human would have no right to repeat. Oh yes, let's not forget the messenger of Satan that God allowed to harass me daily so I would not become conceited or think of myself more highly than I should. I pleaded with the Lord three times to take it away, but He said, His grace was all I needed, for in my weakness; His power becomes perfect in me.

Therefore, I now happily boast as I become aware of my failures, so that Christ's power may rest upon me. This is why I take such pleasure in the insults, hardships, and difficulties; for it's all for the cause of Christ. When I am at my weakest, He is at His strongest, and His grace makes me more than a conqueror.

Conversion and Mission

The day my life changed, was the day I was traveling from Jerusalem to Damascus. I was carrying in my possession letters of imprisonment for all who spoke the name of Jesus. A very horrific encounter came upon me and literally threw me to the ground, leaving me blinded for three whole days.

Filled of egotistical pride, and having complete authority to put all followers in chains, I thought I was totally in control! Little did I realize the fate of the gospel would truly be in the hands of one such as me! I was the one who would now proclaim and die for the very words that once I thought were my enemy.

It was just outside the gate to the city; I remember it clearly! A bright light shown all around me when some strange power knocked me to the ground! Those traveling with me said they heard a noise, but saw nothing! As I lay helpless, as in a trance, unable to move, a voice spoke out of the heavens! For what seemed as hours, but was only minutes, the voice continued to speak; in amazement, I listened? The voice said it was the same Jesus, whom I was persecuting! Then after a period of instructions, including going into the city where I would find a special messenger who would tell me what I was to do next, I regained my composure, and I quickly obeyed. What seemed to me then, a horrifying experience, I was blinded by that light! I was unable to see anything for three whole days! Being distressed by not being able to see, I ate or drank nothing!

Unknowing to me, at that time, there was a disciple of this Jesus, named Ananias living within the city of Damascus. He also received instructions in a vision concerning my situation and was to locate where I was staying. When Ananias received his vision, I too saw as a vision, a man coming to greet me. He was to put his hands upon my head and pray that my sight would return.

Ananias shared later that he was terrified with the thought of coming into my presence. He heard of my mission to persecute all believers of Jesus. The Lord assured him He had chosen me to carry His name to the gentiles and to kings, and to all the descendants of Israel spreading the good news of His grace.

I was anxious, anticipating his arrival to lay hands upon me. When he did, he said, the same Jesus that appeared to me on the road to Damascus sent him so that I may see once more and receive the Holy Spirit. When his hands touched my head, the darkness fell from my eyes! I could see once again! Immediately, I knew this was the power of God! To testify to this miracle, I decided by baptism, to show all I have decided to follow the same Jesus, whom I was determined to condemn. Wanting to make an outward showing of my change in spirit and mind, I decided to stay in Damascus for several days proclaiming Jesus in their synagogues.

All who heard me speak were astonished at the dramatic change in my life. Many asked with much curiosity, if I was the same man who, in Jerusalem, harassed all who called after the name of Jesus. Embarrassed, but confident, I accepted their criticism and understood their concerns.

My First Sermon

I remember my first sermon after the Lord visited me; I was nervous, but excited! I reminded my fellow Jews how in the days of old, God removed King Saul and made David their king. From King David's descendants, this same Jesus came, which God promised and brought to Israel as their Savior. I told them to remember John the Baptist preaching the message of repentance to all Israel saying; he was not the Savior, but He was soon to come.

I preached the good news boldly saying; this message of salvation is to you, the Jew first! Not knowing who He was, they condemned Him to death utterly fulfilling the words from the prophets whom we read every Sabbath. Although they found no reason to sentence Him, they begged Pilate to have Him executed anyway! Then taking Him down from the cross and placing Him in an empty tomb, they unknowingly fulfilled all prophecy.

God raised Jesus from the dead, never to experience decay again. Therefore, they needed to understand that through Him, the forgiveness of sin is proclaimed.

As the meeting at the synagogue ended, and I was leaving, many followed me. They began begging me to continue the message of grace at the next scheduled Sabbath meeting.

At the next meeting, almost the whole town gathered to hear the word of the Lord. When the unbelieving Jews saw the great crowds, they became jealous and objected to the statements that I was making. I stood firm and bold! I declared again the message from Christ! Jesus had made me a light to the Jews first, but since they rejected it and considered themselves unworthy of eternal life, I was instructed to take the gospel unto the Gentile nation. When the crowed heard me say these words, the Gentiles began shouting and glorified the word of the Lord, and all who had believed, received!

Preaching Only Good News

The word of the Lord continued to spread like a wild fire throughout the whole region! There were a few self-righteous Jews who stirred up some high social women along with many male officials who also wanted me to leave. Therefore, I shook the dust off my feet in protest against them and went on to another location to preach (*Acts 3: 22-38*).

In spite of the harassment of my fellow Jewish brothers, I grew more and more powerful in the Spirit of the Lord and continued confounding the Jews through the wisdom of God. Great signs and wonders proved that His grace was upon me. Jesus was truly the Christ, whom they had crucified, and I continued to preach and teach that good news! God's eternal graces from my experience at the gate of Damascus to my final days in the confines of Rome were the best years of my life!

Avoid anyone creating divisions and oppositions! Their only concern is with their own personal needs, which do not serve our Lord. You must be well versed in the doctrine that I teach! Be wise to what is correct and full of grace, remembering the grace of our Lord Jesus Christ is always in you.

There are fourteen epistles accredited to my name, but the letters to the Church at Rome are among my most precious memories."

16 | Legacy of Grace

Chapter Two

Transforming Grace

No Other Gospel

A pastor was preaching a sermon from the book of Romans Chapter 1, and verse 16, "*For I am not ashamed of the gospel, because it is God's power for the salvation of everyone who believes.*" On this particular Sunday morning, the pastor noticed an unfamiliar face in his congregation. The young man was intensely listening to what he had to say about "justification by faith." After the close of service, the pastor met the man and thanked him for choosing their place of worship. The Pastor asked where he was from, and how long he had been serving the Lord. The visitor quickly said he was just passing through to another location, but felt a compelling need to visit his church. To the question of how long he has been a Christian; he looked at his watch and replied, "Oh, I guess about ten minutes now." The message of grace was for this young man, truly a "life-changing event."

The study of God's grace has radically transformed many throughout the pages of time. History reveals a man named St. Augustine was first of those recorded. St. Augustine became changed by the simple message of God's grace.

While visiting with an old friend, Augustine began contemplating his past, considering a life-changing spiritual decision. St. Augustine heard, in the distance, a young child singing lyrics from a hymn; the words invited him to "Take up and read." He noticed a scroll lying nearby, which contained the words from Paul's Roman epistle, Chapter 13, verses, 13-14. Picking it up, he read, "*Let us behave decently, as people who live within the light of the day. No wild parties, drunkenness, sexual immorality, promiscuity, rivalry, or jealousy! Instead, clothe yourselves with the Lord Jesus Christ, and do not obey your flesh and its desires.*"

St. Augustine said he had no need to read past versus 13 and 14. "It was as if a clear light flooded his heart, and all the darkness of doubt vanished away, Augustine said." Those words of the apostle Paul to the people of Rome had a lasting impact on St. Augustine's life as well as the world. St. Augustine stands as a powerful advocate for the accepted belief of Christianity as the only door to the administration of Gods redeeming grace. Soon after his conversion, he was ordained a presbyter. Augustine later took the position as a bishop in the year 396, a position held to his death.

Another life radically changed during the year 1515; a professor named Martin Luther; an Augustinian monk began a study of the letters of the apostle Paul. He especially studied the book of Romans, and taught his findings to his students. Luther recognized justification before God, by faith, through Christ, was a crucial teaching. Luther's study realized a definite need to further the real meaning of Christian life. At first, Luther had a personal struggle with the theme of "grace by faith."After a thorough study, he was totally convinced and the rest is history.

Luther also discovered one particular thread of expression throughout every epistle, "God's righteousness through faith." He realized when our faith mixed with God's faith, revealed God's true plan for man. Luther said God's message of grace was his doorway into heaven.

Two hundred years now pass and this same revelation of grace dramatically changed another pioneer of faith by the name of John Wesley.

While listening to an explanation of how God grace works through faith in Christ, he said he suddenly felt strangely warm. Wesley said he felt a deep assurance he had never felt before. He felt that Christ had truly taken away all his sin, and delivered him from the law of spiritual death.

Not everyone may experience this same dramatic feeling as those great men of God. However, no matter how emotional or mundane your encounter may have been; the work of grace is complete!

Myself included, along with many reliable Bible scholars are virtually unanimous in favor of the overwhelming significance and contribution Paul's writings have upon the foundation of Christ's glorious Church.

Luther's opinion of Paul's letter to the Romans should be the principle book of the New Testament. Not only should every Christian be aware of every word, but also meditate its words regularly. It is as daily bread to the soul, the more time one spends in it, the more precious it becomes; the clearer it appears. Luther spoke as if it were the light leading into all divine mysteries of scripture.

What is it about this mysterious message that affects the lives of so many? Is it its vast treasure to those that plunge deep into its depth, searching, and finding its favor? I agree with Martin Luther that the Legacy of Grace is the only entrance into heaven itself. This mysterious force behind this radical message is, Christ, His undeserved favor from heaven, and once you enter His kingdom; you have His undivided attention and favor forever.

Some very powerful words express the feelings toward any future misunderstandings that might affect this gospel of grace. Paul states, "What I have said in the past, I am now telling you again! If anyone proclaims a gospel contrary to what you received, let that person be judged!"*(Galatians1: 8-9)* As in our present day, some spoke a perverted message with a goal to distort the truth.

Paul proclaimed so boldly and fully, if another gospel is taught, simply don't listen to it! Christ is the only way to salvation! No other door into heaven exists!

Any other gospel would be the imagination of man's ideas and deeds. These would conclude ideas of not approaching God in faith through Christ. Man has the idea that in order to please God; one must sacrifice small children, crawl over sharp objects, or pierce the flesh, anything to show an act of a humility through personal suffering. Man's efforts of penitence to show faith are not acts pleasing to God.

There is a sincere sense of guilt placed upon anyone who seeks to satisfy his or her own philosophical beliefs. Denying God's way of justification is not submitting to the righteousness He assigned. This religious thinking is a mixture of pious ideologies. Mixing oil with water, Christianity with Judaism, or law with grace, the results are the same, spiritual adultery through rebellion!

Paul supports his proclamation by saying, if an angel from heaven or I preached any other message; it would be a lie. It just seems logical, as well as scriptural that all New Testaments disciples be in agreement with Paul's gospel! Paul's message was the direct and personal view from God unto him (*Romans 2:16, 16:25, two Timothy 2:8*).

The Gospel of grace is heaven's number one answer to earth's number one problem; this Gospel is "His legacy!" It is "His will!" Backed by the Holy Spirit, the good news is a gracious divine revelation to all generations who seek the truth. We must never neglect to parallel any Biblical doctrine with Paul's gospel. If you seek to understand the depth of God's grace, it will guard you and keep you from any false doctrine.

Chapter Three

The Gospel, What Is It?

The study of grace brings you into a higher heavenly dimension. Your speech will change; your prayers will change, and your complete Christian outlook on life itself will change. Words like, "God is able" will become, "and God has already given me everything pertaining to life and Godliness" (*Psalms 37:4; One Peter 1:3:4*). The qualification is to "Delight in the Lord." Delighting yourself under the Old Covenant was by works, but under your New Covenant, it is through faith through the blood of Christ.

The messages of grace, contains the A B C of all Christian educations: **A** (*agree*) **B** (*believe*) **C** (*confess*). Until the teaching of God's grace, by faith, through Christ, is voiced, we will remain ignorant of our true Christian heritage and promises (*Hosea 4:6*). The apostle Paul believed the teaching of God's grace must be paramount of all church doctrine, and studied by every believer in order to be holy (set apart) and unashamed before God.

The legacy of grace is God's message revealed to the apostle Paul. Man's right position unto God the Father, by faith through the death and resurrection of His Son, Jesus Christ. Our faith can't be based upon human wisdom, but only upon God's authority (*One Corinthians 2:5*).

In reaction to Adam's rebellion, God pronounced His wrath upon all humanity, and all humanity became sinful as Adam. However, through Christ, He has pronounced all humanity, righteous as Christ. When Jesus died, He canceled our your debt (penalty of sin) with its legal decrees. All its regulations, all its demands which were against us were cleared; we were cursed by association. Humanity was dead to God's favor, but now we are alive (reunited) with Him as He forgave us all of our offenses, erasing the charges brought against us with their decrees. He took those charges away by nailing them to the cross (*Colossians 2:13-14*).

Restoration for humanity is a fact! The new believer has internal employment with eternal enjoyment.

Our justification is in Christ, in His death and resurrection and no other. Once separated by a veil of sin, we are now able to move freely within His domain. We become sinless, and the righteousness of God in Christ.

The Kingdom of God

A kingdom is simply a king's territory, a sovereign government affecting its people to the will and purpose to the king. The king produces a certain culture of values, morals, and lifestyle that affects the heart of its domain. All society living under and in the dominated territory must reflect the desires of its king. The very heart of a kingdom is its king.

God's kingdom is His governmental rule from heaven; brought to earth. Adam was to be His rule on earth; kingdom partners in government, a theocratic order of rule. The kingdom of heaven became the kingdom of God on earth. The right of ownership is the intent and product of the king. The king displays his will on the people. The king has all authority; no one has more authority than its king does. A king's authority is by birth or conquest.

A king also has the authority to give his kingdom to whomever he chooses, allow anyone's audience before him, and give his favor to whomever he pleases. An individual who has favor with the king is considered in "right standing before the throne" or in a righteous position!

Understanding the concepts of the Kingdom of God will help you see more clearly the legacy given its citizens. Christ asked the Jews to pray for His Kingdom to reenter the earth's domain, seek His Kingdom first.

King David said, "The law of the Lord is perfect, restoring the whole person. The testimony of the Lord is sure, making wise simple. The precepts of the Lord are right, rejoicing the heart; the commandment of the Lord is pure and bright, enlightening the eyes.

The reverent fear of the Lord is clean, enduring forever; the ordinances of the Lord are true and righteous altogether. Additionally, by them is your servant warned, reminded, illuminated, and instructed; and in keeping them, there is a great reward (*Psalm 19:7-9, 11,* Amplified).

The welfare among the people is a reflection of its king. A true king is a loving king. The more prosperous the kingdom, the more attractive to those seeking a new habitation, and the more newcomers will want to join its domain. Every born-again believer is a kingdom citizen who has changed his or her dwelling and lifestyle according to King Jesus. A kingdom is its king; his words are its laws; the king is its constitution.

Kingdom Welfare

We read an account in Matthew's gospel, of a man in need of healing who had a flesh disfiguring disease called leprosy. The man asks Jesus "if" He would heal him. The question denotes doubt! Possibly, He will, but maybe, He won't! Jesus replied with a simple, "I will; go be clean!" This opens the question of His ability versus His willingness (*Matthew 8:3*). How many Christians have said, "Well, if it's Gods will; He will heal me." If we can read, we should know if it's Gods will or not! This is why He sent His Holy Spirit, to teach us the will of the Father. Humans don't like to admit their unbelief, so we want to place the burden upon God by religiously using the words, "if it be God's will." Then if not delivered, we can always say, "it must have not been His will, after all, His ways are far beyond our ways." Oh, that sounds humble, so religious, yet so blinded by self. It wouldn't be politically correct to say dumb, would it?

Let's view it in this manner; if you went to your local bank and asked for a loan, being in the lending business, you would expect their "ability" to be matched by your equity. Are they willing to grant you the necessary funds you asked for? The answer solely depends upon "you're personal" merits; you're worth. You may qualify for only a lesser amount than asked, due to your equity. God's gift of grace, on the other hand, is upon His equity and brings His blessings of abundant life, solely upon "His willingness." Nothing is upon your merits!

Your God is not only able, but He is very much willing, regardless of your ability to repay, for you have no ability to repay. He has willed to give you the kingdom. He said it was His Father's pleasure to give us, His kingdom. When you became a kingdom citizen, you receive His ability together with His willingness, but we must take the kingdom by force, the force of faith. Faith takes, and doubt does without (*Luke 12:32*).

Jesus said there was never anyone born greater than John the Baptist was. How can the least important person in His kingdom be finer than John was? How can this be possible?

Jesus said, "From the days of John the Baptist until the present, the kingdom of heaven has been forcefully advancing, and violent people have been attacking it. For the Law and all the Prophets prophesied up to the time of John" (*Matthew 11:11 – 13*, emphasis added). John's death was a shadow of the law passing away, for Jesus said, "up to the time of John."

None was greater than John the Baptist. It is all because of His grace! Grace is greater than the law was. John lived within the law of works, and the law represents the teachings of Moses. Grace represents the teachings of Christ. If ever faced with a test, which life coach would you be more comfortable? John preached the baptism of repentance, but Jesus preached faith in His Father.

Our earthly governments get their authority from the people or an act of violence. On the other hand, our authority is from the King Himself. A believer who lives a faith lifestyle is the total opposite of the world's view of a violent lifestyle. The kingdom "suffers (affirms) violence" (pressure to be seized), and the force of pressure is the "affirmation" to those applying their faith. Storming the kingdom is boldly going where no human has ever gone; grace allows the personally taking of what rightly belongs to you; enjoying your legacy.

The strong and forceful, which apply the "pressure of faith" upon heaven's judicial system, will eagerly seize and carry off their booty. The kingdom of God operates on a "FAITH COME; FAITH SERVED" basis. We must confess to confirm!

Once Controlled

According to the gospel of Jesus and of Paul, we are free from the law. We are by grace spiritually dead to what once controlled and held us captive. We no longer are to serve under obedience to a Task Master of written regulations. We are to serve under willingness for obeying the prompting of the Holy Spirit in a newness of life (*Romans 7:6*).

The Ten Commandments, i.e. the law, only allows man to connect with God through the acts of his or her self-worth, but our New Covenant connection is through Christ's blood. By no other act of human involvement except the trust in His Word can we become righteous enough to present ourselves before Him.

This legacy is not a brand-new law, a fresh code of ethics, or an unknown set of moral standards! It is not a refreshed doctrine, a new religion, or just some ethical earthly advice to live by! This Gospel is the "genuine good news" the "Legacy of Grace" is God's divine last will and testament connecting between heaven and earth, kingdom to kingdom. The law was humanity communicating to God, but grace is God communicating to man.

This gospel of grace is God's significant point of view towards His creation. This view involves special persons of interest as an act of His Father's excellent pleasure. Jesus Himself bestowed this legacy upon all humanity. The kingdom of Heaven now becomes the kingdom of God in all believers. God's legacy of Grace, is His undeserved favor given to all, a decree of loving-kindness; paid for with his blood! A legacy is defined as a grant given to someone deemed worthy by the giver; a birthright, an inheritance, a bequest, a heritage; free to the receiver, but very costly to the donor.

Prodigal World

Because of Adam's rebellion, spiritual separation gave way to physical death and ruled through his sin. By receiving God's grace, humanity can righteously reign in this life once again! (*Romans 5:17*)

All humanity sinned and fell short of God's honor and glory, which is the death and resurrection of His dear Son. All now are justified and made upright and in right standing with Him. All this is made possible, and freely by His grace, His mercy and unmerited favor through the redemption provided in Christ Jesus (*Romans 3:23-24*). Humanity did nothing to deserve the penalty of Adam's sin, but all became sinners. Humanity also has done or can do nothing to deserve the gift of God's grace, but we have all become righteous through Christ. Since we had nothing to do with Adam's transgression, but suffered its curse, we have also nothing to do with the transaction of grace, but to enjoy its freedom.

The firstborn brother in the book of Luke, Chapter 15, represents the law. The older son, as does the law, sees the rebellion (sin) as a traitor, but grace sees the rebellion as childish immaturity. A rebellious son returns from his unprotected life; returning to the protection of a loving father, this was all the remorse the father needed.

Neither the earthly father nor the heavenly Father condoned the actions of either wayward child. The household suffered emptiness. Both wasted their birthright. Both chose to separate from their birth father and live in the nakedness of an unprotected environment. Both remained immensely loved and very much related regardless of their transgression.

Repentance merely means to think differently, change direction, reconsider, and feel compunction morally (Strong's Concordance). Repentance is not simply saying, I'm sorry, then returning to the same unrighteous lifestyle. The prodigal showed true repentance by a 180-degree turn in the opposite direction, a return home.

Notice the five (number for grace) positions that the father took toward restoration. While the son was still far away, his father (1) saw him, (2) was filled with compassion, (3) ran to his son, (4) threw his arms around him, and (5) kissed him affectionately. (*15:20*)

Our Own Children

In the rearing of children, as they grow into maturity, sometimes may act disrespectful, become rebellious, cheat, or even lie. I know I'm speaking of someone else's child, but some may have even run away from home, breaking all communications. When found, some may have said, I am sorry, but what they might be saying is, "I'm sorry you caught me!"

I'm sure of this reaction, if admitted, is a memory of most of us, and fearing the consequence of parental wrath, crying and begging of forgiveness would follow. Some were Oscar winners, but then quickly "slide back," repeating their rebellious actions again.

There must be a heart change (inner conscience change) if truly repentant.

In spite of their unruly emotions, did they remain your children, even though the thought of disowning them might have crossed your mind? Keep in mind, God is our father figure; His parental handling is our guide.

When they disobeyed repeatedly, did their youthful, self-willed rebellion wipe out their DNA? You knew, by experience; at their age, they should be more mature, and act within the knowledge, of whom and whose they were, but a loving hope caused patience to have its perfect work, waiting in rest for that special day of growth. For most of us, it finally arrived.

In our modern court system, a person can annul their relationships by a decree from the courts, but heaven's judicial system doesn't operate as such. Sin was and is the only separation between God and humanity.

What responsible parent disowns their child? We have earthly laws that forbid abandonment and child abuse, but we treat our heavenly Father as if He were a spiritual child abuser! He is the supreme father example, and yet we want to place Him in our mental arena. Do you really think that your heavenly Father is as negligent, unforgiving, or sinful as we are? What about the adopted child, do they become "un-adopted" because they rebel and stray off into their own ways? The adopted child should have more legal rights than a birth child, for they were chosen.

Growth Process

We, who are in Christ, by adoption, are chosen; now belonging to the royal kingdom family of heaven and given a legacy as an inheritance, although Satan may detest it, he can never revoke it!

Growth is a process and sometimes a few wrong decisions, a few bad mistakes; a few missing the mark will cause communication gaps. We as parents, place before our children mental road signs, but do they always follow your directions? What about those terrible twos, or the nerve bending teen years we thought, as parents would never end. Reminded again of a phrase from my youth, "you don't throw out the clean baby with the filthy bath water." Does God cast you away when you fall, hurt yourself on the rocks of life, and get dirty? No, He runs to you, has compassion, embraces you, and treats you with loving affections. Washes you, nourishes you, treating you as if you never missed His will!

Humanity is living in a lost world, due to Adam, living in a sinful state of affairs. Therefore, the whole of humanity is out of the Father's protection, as was the prodigal. Christ has welcomed back all of humanity and as a whole, no longer lost; just a few stragglers still groping through the darkness outside His kingdom, those who have not yet claimed their pardon. I'm reminded of a movie I once saw, "The Living Dead." Zombies were walking through the streets of towns, arms outstretched, searching for life.

Family of God

Humanity was that prodigal of whom Jesus spoke, a rebellious child, due to the act of treason against the Father. The wasteful son, as a missing sheep or a misplaced coin all are types of an unrighteous world, out of fellowship, out of relationship.

Jesus said there is great joy in the presence of angels over one sinner who changes his mind and turns from his rebellion. We as born-again believers are not sinners! We may miss God a few times, okay, maybe more than a few times, but you are not practicing the evil art of sinning, are you?

Are we the believer, the blood cleansed, still sinners? Wait a minute; was not all our sin washed away in the flow of His blood? Then why do some of us almost boast of still being sinners? It might be religious, but it's not Biblical! We have no residue of past sins clinging to our spirits! It makes me think like a man who cut his face shaving and has multiple pieces of tissue all over his face. Washed means, water applied, clean means cleansed! There is no leaving His fold, He is the door, and if you want to stray, you must pass through Him! If you want to leave His protection, you must willingly escape!

I believe there are "Children of God" today, living as spiritually homeless, living in sinful conditions, wandering the streets of the kingdom living under a hopeless condemnation, all because some religious individual said they were backslid, disowned by their heavenly Father, and separated by their failures.

You may mentally wander from the fold, but you are still His lamb. You are a free moral being. You may miss the Fathers wishes, but you are still born of Him.

Are His rod and His staff a means of punishment or a comforting restraint? The characteristic of sheep is not too smart and easily led away to destruction. Some shepherds would sleep at the gate of the sheepfold to protect the sheep from their personal demise. Some would even break the leg of a self-willed sheep to stop it from following their particular dumb curiosities, becoming lost and unprotected.

Reminded of Paul's teaching in Hebrews, Chapters 5 and 6, he instructs the converted Jew concerning their lack in spiritual hearing and their laziness in achieving any unworldly revelation. Even though they should have been teaching others, they actually were in need of someone teaching them again of the very first values of God's Word. He said they were as infants on milk, unable to consume solid food, saying, everyone who continues to feed on milk is obviously inexperienced and unskilled in knowing his or her "rightful position" to the divine will and purpose in Christ. Their thoughts and actions were as newborn babies; too young even to speak their faith. He says solid food is for those whose senses and mental faculties are trained by practice to classify and distinguish between what is morally good and upright and what is evil and contrary either to divine or human law.

Therefore, we need to grow up and get past the elementary teachings and doctrine of grace in Christ. We should be growing steadily toward the completeness and perfection that belong in spiritual maturity. We should be looking beyond the doctrines of repentance and forsaking all dead works of the law, growing even beyond the faith that caused us to receive Christ.

The doctrine of baptisms and immersions of the body in water, the sprinklings, and washings were common religious rites among the Hebrews. The doctrine of placing on of the hands was frequent, especially in acts of sacrifices: the person bringing the sacrifice laid his hands on the animal's head, confessing his sins over it, and then giving it to the priest to offer before God, that it might make atonement for his transgressions. This as well had respect to Jesus Christ, that Lamb of God who takes away the sins to the world. The doctrine of the resurrection of the dead and of eternal judgment, were also Jewish law.

Paul continues to explain how once a mature child is enlightened, who has consciously accepted the heavenly gift of grace through the Holy Spirit, and knows how well the Word of God is, "if they turn backward under the law, turn away from their allegiance of faith in Christ, it is impossible to bring them back to repentance." He explains that in doing so, they make the cross of no effect.

Paul says, "If they fell back," he didn't say they would fall into their old way of life; this is as to say, if you jumped from a cliff, you would most likely die, so don't take the leap!

This would be as nailing Christ afresh upon the cross and holding Him in contempt and a public showing of shame of disgrace. God is not pleased with that stage of rebellion. Those who do such things of their own free will, "have no heart to repent."

As we grow in grace, we rebel to a lesser degree and stray not as much. We conduct ourselves as mature children. David said the Lord is our shepherd, to lead, feed, guide, and shield from any harm. He makes us lie rested in green pastures besides peaceful waters. Not by our own efforts, but for His namesake, He leads us in paths of righteousness, where we are to fear no evil. When we follow Gods wishes more and more, and trust in His directions, we will bear the fruit of repentance. Goodness and mercy will follow us all the days of our life, and He will bless us in the view of all our enemies *(Psalm 23:1-5)*.

God does not physically nor spiritually break the legs of His children to keep us in His fold. His ways of keeping us in His care is beyond our human thinking, but is not to harm us in any way. *"For I know the thoughts and plans that I have for you, says the Lord, thoughts and plans for* **welfare and peace** *and* **not for evil**, *to* **give you hope** *in your final outcome"* (*Jeremiah 29:11*, Amplified, emphasis added).

East and West

I was recently reading, Psalm Chapter 103, verse 12, and thinking about the blueprint of the tabernacle in the wilderness. It awakened my thinking to the reality of this phrase, "As far as the East is from the West." This is not just a global distance between two earthly points, but also the distance between the burnt offering and the Ark of the Covenant. *"As far as the east is from the west, He has removed our transgressions."* From the spilling of blood at the East entrance, to the covering of sins by the sprinkling of blood for Atonement upon the Ark at the West end of the tabernacle, we now have no sinful connection. Knowing there is also no global connection between the east and the west, the two never meet.

Many have quoted the scripture from the book of Numbers, chapter 32, and verse 23 (Amplified), *Behold; you have sinned against the Lord and be sure your sin will find you out."* This passage has nothing to do with your New Covenant relationship. Your past sin not at any time will ever find you or meet up with your present grace! Jesus is recorded in the gospel of John as saying, *"I give them eternal life, and* **they will never perish**, *and* **no one will snatch them out of my hand"** *(John 10:28,* emphasis added).

Seen in these next few words, is a magnificent insight of Christ's pure grace; for this is how God so loved the world. He gave his unique Son so that everyone who believes in Him might not be destroyed, but have eternal life" *(John 3:16)*.

When you do a word search within the meaning of "perish" and "eternal life," you will find it referring to a life of restoration, a reconnecting, or "placing back" as if there were never any breach of contract. This action is an everlasting, a never-ending, irrevocable event, and that my friend, is amazing grace and good news; this is the Gospel.

If a book fell, and you wanted to "re-place" it to its original position, would you place it anywhere other than its designated shelf? No, you would "restore" to its "first position." This is where God has placed you. He has picked you up, not only dusting you off, but also washed you, and placed you back into a Garden Righteous position. God sees you as if at no time disobedient, as if you did not once fall short of His grace. You repented; you changed your mind concerning sin and your disobedience toward your heavenly Father and now are to rest in His ability to sustain you.

The spectrum of God's love is immeasurable, far beyond any compassionate thinking, confounding all human reasons that some have followed atheism of agnosticism. If you can't see it, feel it, taste it, hear it, or smell it, then it doesn't exist, therefore, there is no God!

God didn't see just one wayward soul, but an entire lost world. He foresaw a world of righteous sons and daughters, and this caused our heavenly Father to be ecstatic about the death and resurrection of His Son Jesus. This was the reinstatement plan of God's grace upon the earth, a welcoming home with open arms party. Children of God could now come back into the domain of the king and re-establish their original royal position.

Jesus resurrecting a dead world back to spiritual life, and that made all heaven rejoice. One missing member, one lost sheep, or one misplaced coin; all are lost; as lost as Adam in the garden after his rebellion: the Lord God called to Adam, *"Adam, where are you?"* (*Genesis 3:9*)

Some say we are all God's children. True we are all His creations, but the only way you can become a son or daughter, is through a grace relationship. Children are in name only, but the birth child is more accessible to all the father's possessions. Although my neighbor's child is a human, and may be adorable, he or she is not my child, and I don't treat that child as I would my own.

We as "born-again" believers are favored children through the birth of divine grace and therefore, called sons. *"As many as receive Him, to them, He gave power to become the sons of God, even to them that believe on His name. Behold what manner of love the Father hath bestowed upon us to be the sons of God. Therefore, the world knows us not, because it knew Him not. Now we are the sons of God, and it does not yet appear what we shall be: but we know that, when He shall appear, we shall be like Him;* **for we shall see Him as he is.***"* This means, *"As He is* **so are we** *in this world"* (Romans 8:14; John 1:12; 1 John 3:1-2, 4:17 KJV, emphasis added). We were complete in Him and when He returns, He will see His people as spotless, and sanctified as He.

The apostle Paul wrote to the new believers at Ephesus, which applies to us today, saying, we were dead (separated) from God because of our sin. We were once living according to the lifestyle of this present world, following the lusts of our flesh, fulfilling its desires and senses. Satan, the ruler of the power over the air, was active in us who were disobedient to the gift of grace.

We became deceived and ruled by our sinful nature deserving, His wrath, but God, even when we were out of His relationship, because of His mercy and great love for humanity, made us alive again and seated us together with Christ. He placed us in the heavenly realm with Him, in Christ Jesus, to show His richness of grace and kindness toward us.

We have salvation only through our faith and not of personal works, lest anyone be tempted to brag of their righteousness. This grace does not come from us; this is His legacy.

Paul teaches that we, the born-again believer, are Christ's masterwork, people created for valid works not from proper works. We were destined long before we were born. We are not to forget that at one time we were all sinners by birth. We were without Christ, excluded from citizenship, outside the kingdom and strangers to the Commonwealth of promise. We were in a world without God, but now restored to a relationship by His blood.

Christ made the law inoperative, along with its commandments and regulations. He created in Himself, a brand-new humanity, a fresh kingdom citizen, the children of God. Christ reconciled all, to God in one body through the cross, on which His hostility toward humanity also died. We now have access to the Father in one Spirit. This is why we are no more strangers to God, no longer pilgrims looking for a dwelling, but kingdom citizens, members of God's household (*Ephesians 2:1-20*).

Chapter Four

Starting Point of Grace

The good news of God's legacy is your life after His death; the starting point of Grace, you're beginning with no end.

The message of grace sets forth a fulfillment of promises by the prophets of old. This Divine master plan meticulously thought out before the foundation of all things, was set in motion by the king of heaven Himself. A plan that speaks of Jesus being the Christ, the Savior, the Son of God, the Promised One; He who came from King David as to His human nature, but rising from the dead, and declared the Son of God, by His Divine power. The Christian profession doesn't consist in academics or empty approvals, but lives within the obedience to the voice of faith.

We are of the family of God, many citizens making up the colony of Christ. *(Romans Chapter 12, One Corinthians Chapter 12)* By acknowledging God's grace to sanctify our reasoning, we have His peace to comfort our minds as He reconciles all believers through Christ unto Himself *(Romans 5:10, Two Corinthians 5:18-20, Colossians 1:21)*.

We should never find ourselves embarrassed of the gospel. God's grace declares and establishes the rules as a basis of argument for all deliverance. The gospel is the "power of God unto salvation" for everyone who believes. This is the prerequisite for righteousness; God revealed in us. The words of faith are within our words. His faith mixed with our faith. The righteous will live by faith *(Romans 16-17)*.

God's gospel is our only common hope for pure righteousness. Receive it and seize it, snooze and lose it! Let's remember, since it may have escaped some; the Gospel of salvation, which if you have welcomed and accepted, rests upon your individual faith, your personal words, and if you hold on and do not waiver, grace will be with you all the days in your life (*One Corinthians 15:1-2*).

How many unconsciously, at one time or another, acted ashamed of His gospel? Embarrassed maybe due to unanswered prayer, allowing condemnation because of a lack of confidence in God, to creep in and fill your hearts. We may think, "How can I be a good witness if God does not even answer my requests?" The further we trust Him, the more we receive from Him. We aren't given a choice; we are to live by trusting in God; we can't develop a rich Christian life by physical power, it' must be totally by His Spirit (*Zechariah 4:6*).

The Now Faith

Faith is now! (*Hebrews 11:1*) What does this mean? Faith is always seeing what God declared as your destiny, existing in your now of time. Tomorrow it may be Saturday, but when Saturday arrives, it is currently, today. There is no time realm with God, He lives outside time, so He is constantly in your current moment; we walk by faith; we walk as if it is in the moment, because we take hold of it at present time, not by sight; sight is always future (*two Corinthians 5:7*).

Faith is our title deed to any scriptural reference in God's Word. According to heaven, if you can believe it, you will own it, and if you will own it, you see it!

Your contract is sealed with the king's signet, written with His blood, backed by the Supreme Court Judge of the Universe. He who cannot lie, all ruling is in your favor; yes and so be it, it is finished, and you are complete, for in Him; His grace is sufficient, in the now!

You might think there are none justified before God, all have wronged Him (*Romans 3:10*). If you think about it, it sounds somewhat depressing. No one able to approach God, no one good enough to have His favor; this is what was, but not what is in the now.

Paul expressed his desire for the spiritual deliverance of his own people, who, having a zeal for God, had no knowledge of the truth: They sought their salvation by personal fleshly works, not by faith in Christ. No one recognized or comprehended the truth. No one sought out God. All turned away, together becoming unprofitable and worthless: No one doing right, not even one! (*Romans 3:11-12*)

When the words, "has, have, or had" are used, it is always referring to the past. The reference Paul uses, that all "have" sinned, and "have" come short of God's glory, is speaking of the past. Paul didn't say, all are sinning and all are missing God's glory. The glory that the world had come concise of was the glory God's restoration. By accepting God's plan of redemption, we don't come short any longer, for we have hit the BULLS EYE by seeking His kingdom first, and receiving His righteousness. The kingdom of God is the Kingdom of Righteousness. The Holy Spirit is His righteous kingdom; His kingdom is His domain, where the Spirit of the Lord is, His kingdom is, and therefore, His kingdom has come, and we have its liberties.

Kingdom citizens are supposed to reflect their king. They are to show what their king is like, by the way, they live, act, dress, walk, and talk. They are to reflect the nature and character of their king. Our heavenly King is righteous, just, compassionate, and generous. This is why there is no poverty in the kingdom of Heaven, no economic turmoil, and no shortage of any type. As King David declared it so strongly, he had never seen a kingdom citizen forsaken or their children begging for food (*Psalm 37:17, 25*).

I mentioned in my last book, "Declaring Justice," God's glory was what He does, the characteristics of a creator, but I would like to extend that thought further to His Son Jesus, the Christ. Christ is truly the glory of God, His crowning achievement. The world, due to Adam, fell from grace. Falling away is another way of saying they missed their calling or their desired intended position.

Righteousness according to the law demands a right position of perfect obedience to its rules. The gospel of Grace demands a walk by faith, and obedience to its law.

The intent behind the law was to reveal man's failure toward God, not a mere perception, but a true acquaintance with sin, which works toward repentance, faith, and a holy character. Grace is unconnected from the Law. As the tree of good and evil in the garden (representing the law), was separate from the tree of life (representing grace), so is righteousness from humanity, but you can't eat from both trees. Grace, unlike the tree, is not forbidden, but unto all who believe, for there is no difference, since we all are under Adam, and all have sinned and fallen short of His honor and glory, but now all are justified through Christ and made upright (righteous) with God; freely, and without any human participation.

God placed Jesus before all, as the true mercy seat, the propitiation for all humanity, by His blood, the last cleansing and life-giving sacrifice of atonement, our reconciliation, received, through faith. This was to show God's personal righteousness, His divine kindness, causing Him to pass over and ignore many past rebellious acts without any wrath or punishment.

Forty years Israel sinfully complained; too cold, as well as hot, complained when they were hungry, and again when they were thirsty. After being delivered from 400-years of bondage, they wished they were back in the hands with their enemy; how disrespectful, but God was graceful to their needs.

God was their 40-year provider. Not one was sick among them; the soles of their shoes didn't wear thin. He was their daily cloud, and their evening fire. He fed them in the morning and evening, and gave them water from a rock just to show them, His loving kindness. All He wanted was their unconditional love in return, but it was humanly impossible to give God something they didn't own (*Exodus 13:21 -22, 16: 3-35, 17:2-7*). All this grace was to demonstrate and prove to the people; He was their present redeemer, their great I Am. Now, you and I, through Christ, are justified, not by our obedience, but by our faith.

Since humans had no part in this form of righteousness, pride and boasting are of no advantage. According to the principle of faith, a person is justified and made upright only by their independent faith and not their good deeds. According to God, any observance of the Law has nothing to do with justification!

Jesus Sealed Your Deal

No personal works of the flesh, called by any name, any shape, or form, have the basis worthy of justification! I don't say Christianity shouldn't produce good works, or that those who are justified shouldn't obey His Law, but no self- righteous endeavors can be sinless enough to produce pure righteousness for a sinful world.

We all were once sinners, without Christ, with no claim to His favors, but His legacy to all humanity speaks loudly; all must be pardoned by faith alone, without any personal works of which we can boast. Again, I have heard some say, we are all sinners; truth is, after Christ, you are either sinless, or you are not. We, as humans, make that statement thinking it is an act of humility, but in reality, it is the doorway leading into a self-righteous attitude, leading to a walk of condemnation, ruled by what our five physical senses dictate to our brain as true religion.

This is the uniqueness of Christianity. Martin Luther often called this doctrine, "the article upon which the church stands or falls." If this doctrine of faith stands as truth, all others must unite with it, but if we neglect such a great salvation, all others will also fall (*Hebrews 2:3*).

This doctrine by no means interferes with the doctrine of good works. We do not become a Christian by performing excellent works, but recognized as Christians by the performance of valid deeds (*One Peter 2:12*). It should be apparent to all, that everyday; your Christian walk has no grounds for justification. Of course, for the unbeliever, this preaching is foolishness, but for us whom believe, it is pure wisdom by God's design. God openly displays the foolishness of this world to show that His ways are much wiser and stronger.

The Jews were for seeking some miraculous sign, and the Greeks were always seeking greater wisdom, but Paul boldly preached only the effects of the cross; Christ crucified, buried, and resurrected. Countless sermons in churches across the globe preach the abuse prior to Christ's death, but few preach the more significant results that are attainable after His death. Christ didn't say; remember His birth, although that is influential. He didn't say to remember His baptism, which is also important. He didn't even say to remember His miracles, but He did say to remember His body, which was broken for us. He also said when we partake of communion to remember His blood sacrifice for us. "As often as you eat the bread, and drink the cup, we show the importance of the Lord's death" (*One Corinthians 11:23-26*).

In Paul's time, the teaching of grace was offensive to the Jews and caused a violent reproach. To the Greeks, it was foolishness, and brought much ridicule. I find it quite amazing that the same results are prevalent of our present day, not a physical attack yet, but one of the ridicule and unbelief. The attacks come from the same religious spirit that plagued the early church, but to us, New Testament believers, there should be no contest to the gospel of Paul's teaching, for it is the same message of Christ. You might say it's all in the interpretation of Scriptures; well, ok, but the message of grace interrupts itself. We are the generation called out and chosen to be a royal priesthood. We are His very own holy people, proclaiming His wonderful grace, delivered out of Spiritual darkness into His marvelous light of revelation. Our only peculiarity, we were sought out and bought, paid for with His blood (*One Peter 2:9*). This is the day of a "Grace Revolution!"

God has always chosen the foolish things from this world to mystify those who are self-exalted. God chooses the weak and simple things of this world to confuse the mighty, so that no flesh can boast of any personal good in His presence. You can't come before His throne and say, Hey, God, look what I have done. It is Christ in us, who of God are made to us His wisdom, His righteousness, His sanctification, and His redemption (past tense). Any who boasts, let them glory in the Lord (*One Corinthians 1:30*). I ask you, how can we read these words and not place all these attributes under the heading of grace?

Christ had faith in His Father's plan, enough that He willingly offered Himself for the world's ransom. If Jesus said we are complete in Him and all He has is within the inheritance to the Saints, we then, have His faith also. That is worth repeating. If we are complete in Christ, we also have His faith. Not only do we have His faith, but also His peace! (*John 14:27*)

This unchanging, unwavering inheritance isn't reserved in heaven waiting on our appearance. It's not, in the sweet, by and by, but it is supported by a glorious command, "we have it now in

Christ." We spend too much time thinking about a beautiful mansion when God wants us blessed in our present time. When Satan brings the pompous, religious idea that God doesn't want you blessed, don't speak your thoughts! *"Therefore, take no thought, saying, what shall we eat? Or what shall we drink? Or, wherewithal shall we be clothed? Take therefore no thought for the morrow: for the morrow shall take thought for the things of itself. Sufficient unto the day is the evil thereof (Matthew 6:31 and 34 KJV).*

Spots, Wrinkles, Blemishes

To the un-renewed mind, the ultimate foolish thought is, how can humanity, be eternally redeemed, put back into a holy position with God, by the simple, extraordinary act, of another human dying upon a wooden cross and shedding blood? You have to admit, sounds astonishing I know, but this is the foolish plan of a very wise creator; it fooled even the devil! *(One Corinthians 2:8)*

Grace is the design to improve our Christian walk. Faith declares openly a method of deliverance from all condemnations, and then builds a foundation upon wholesomeness in the conscience of grateful believers. God is holy and just! What unrighteous mortal, can boldly come before His throne as He bids us to do? *(Hebrews 4:16)* It is necessary that we approach Him with Christ's Holiness, holiness without guilt, past, present, or future.

This positioning of grace is purely available in Christ by faith in His death and resurrection. It is just by His righteousness; we stand guiltless, without spot, wrinkle, or blemish. We are able to stand holy and acceptable before God's infinite satisfaction of sinless grace, sprinkled with sacrificial blood of the Supreme Lamb. He is our Mercy Seat; He is our Lamb, and He is our redemption!

Faith delivers it all, and the last time I looked; all still means all. Your Christian walk is not from "His faith to produce good deeds," as if it was only His faith that placed you into a justified state.

We have His faith, and His faith takes! Christ wants us to become a "by faith taker," taking His faith and applying it to our lives. Paraphrasing what Jesus said in Matthew, Chapter 11, and verse 29, "Take my yoke upon you, learn from me, and I will give you rest for your soul." It was not by the blood of animals that He could enter once into the most Holy Place, obtaining eternal redemption for us, but it was by His own blood once for all! If the ashes and the blood of animals, which sprinkled the unclean, could sanctify our sinful debt, how much more, did the blood of Christ Himself, cleanse our conscience from all dead works? Therefore, at His coming, He will see His people without any spots or blemishes (*Hebrews 9:12-14; two Peter 3:14*). "*Come now, and let us reason together, says Jehovah;* **though your sins are as scarlet, they shall be as white as snow; though they are red like crimson, they shall be like wool**" (*Isaiah 1:18* emphasis added).

Paul writes that Christ will present His church to Himself in glorious splendor, without spot or wrinkle (*Ephesians 5:27*). Many are striving to personally wash and iron out their sinful wrinkles with a self-righteous iron. The good news of the Gospel is, Christ has washed and cleansed all your filthy laundries using the pure miracle stain remover, "FAITHENAL." When you accepted Christ, all your soiled laundries were washed clean! All your personal efforts to straighten your faults were useless and good only in producing condemnation. Your dirty laundry, cannot be cleansed by shouting, praying, or preaching, they have been (past tense) bleached white as the purest snow, by "faith in all" His grace filled works.

I know humanity loves to cry and moan in an effort to move God toward our needs, when, the truth is, He has already given us all things that pertain to natural life and eternal Godliness. Any fleshly tears will not move God or help dissolve away any of life's problems!

I have seen many people over the years come forward in a church service to accept Christ and watched while they cry enough tears to fill buckets, but leaving empty of grace. After easing their guilt, they leave as unclean spiritually as they were when they came forward. They were sorry, for the moment, but there was no heart change.

The book of Ephesians tells us the thief must no longer steal. The filthy talker must clean up his conversation. Stop all bitterness, greed, wrath, anger, quarreling, and slander. Sexual impurity or obscene joking of any kind should not be mentioned among us; totally inappropriate conduct. We are to show a heavenly kindness and compassion toward all as Christ has forgiven us. These acts are not for us to gain God's grace, but are the attributes of His grace in us (*Ephesians 4:28-32; 5:3-4*)

Every high priest, at the time of Moses, was ordained of God for offering gifts and sacrifices before the Lord. It was necessary that Jesus, as our New Testament Priest, have an offering to present also in accordance with the Law of Moses. Priests offered gifts as an outline of what was the true existence and reality in the heavenly sanctuary. When Moses was about to erect the tabernacle, he was instructed to make it exactly to the model, which was shown him on Mount Sinai with God (*Exodus 25:40*). Not to be erected as an exact structure, but exact as in significance and meaning was Jesus our officiating High Priest, seated at the right hand of the Father in heaven, ministering on our behalf (*one John 2:1*).

Christ was given a more exceptional priestly ministry from His heavenly Father, different from the old covenant priesthood. It is more superior and excellent, because it performs and rests upon His righteousness and not any fleshly good deed of His people. The first covenant had faults, if it were not true; there would have been no need for another or any attempt to institute another. However, the Lord showed the inadequacy of the old when He said he would make and ratify a new agreement. Unlike the first, this covenant would be upon the minds among the people, imprinted upon their innermost thoughts and understanding.

God spoke of a brand-new agreement, an alignment between Him and earth; He fulfilled the new, making the first obsolete, and what is obsolete, is annulled because it is out of date, and discarded. The first covenant was filled with rules and regulations, eat this, don't eat that, wear this, but not that. Many today are trying to live their Christian walk by the same rules of an obsolete covenant. By experience, trying to live by rules and regulations will cause a spirit of self-righteous superiority to come upon you, thinking your beliefs are more spiritual than others are, causing a division among the saints. The old covenant had rules for divine worship and a physical sanctuary for a tabernacle. The new covenant has a sanctuary not made by human hands, but a heavenly tabernacle of righteousness.

The New Order

The Holy Spirit pointed the way into the true Holy of Holies. The first tabernacle was a visible picture whose gifts and sacrifices were incapable of perfecting the conscience or of cleansing and renewing any part of the inner man. Its ceremonies dealt only with clean and unclean meats and drinks and different washings; fleshly external rules and regulations, which kept the people sanctified until the time of the complete brand new order, when Christ, established the reality of a fresh and better covenant. This was as a promissory note held until the debt was paid.

Christ is our true High Priest, making a one-time atonement; Christ also is our Ark, housing the safety of His people and our Mercy seat concealing all our failures.

Our negotiator of this entirely new Will and Testament is Christ Himself. We, His children, have received the fulfillment of that promise, our everlasting inheritance, but for a personal will to have any effect, a certification of death must first exist. A will is valid only at death, and has no force of power as long as the one who made it is still alive (*Hebrews 9:16-18*).

Under the Law of Moses, it was necessary to cleanse all the replicas of heavenly things with ceremonial washings. Almost everything was by blood purified, and therefore, the actual blissful things were in need of a righteous sacrifice, too. As Moses would read each command of the law before the people then take the blood of the slain sacrifice, he would sprinkle the book, the tabernacle and the people, along with the sacred vessels and appliances used in divine worship. He would next proclaim these words, "Behold this is the blood of the covenant, which Jehovah has made with you" (*Exodus 24:6-8*).

In Harmony with Grace

Without the shedding of blood, there is neither release nor decrease from any debt due to punishment for sin. Christ didn't enter a sanctuary made by human hands, but He entered into heaven's Holy of Holies, to appear in the presence of God on your behalf, nor did He enter to offer a continual sacrifice every year; repeatedly, as did the earthly high priest. He entered once for all, with His own blood, to put away and abolish all sin by His sacrifice.

Our fleshly bodies are subject to this sin cursed earth, appointed to die once, as Christ also formerly. However, when He died, and took upon Him our death, our sin, beforehand for all! Jesus will appear again, a second and last time, but this time; He will not carry any cross nor deal with anyone's sin. He will bring a full deliverance to the believers who are eagerly waiting and patiently expecting Him. If you are concerned of not being sinless when Christ's returns, He is not coming to deal with your or my sin. When Christ returns, His judgment will be upon the ungodly for rejecting Him; unless you consider yourself anti-God, I wouldn't worry any.

The law was merely a sketch of the good things to come, it at no time, would repeat the same sacrifices continually year after year made anyone perfect enough to approach God. If it were otherwise possible to make one righteous, these sacrifices would have not at any time stopped.

Since now, we have sanctification through the New Birth; we no longer are slaves to a guilt consciousness of sin. There is no need of sacrifices that bring the fresh remembrance of unforgiving sin each year. In harmony with the grace of God, all who believe are set apart from sin.

One Single Offering

Christ, after offering the single sacrifice for our sins, was seated at the right hand (righteousness) of God. Why did, He sit down? Was it because He was tired? No, it was because the supreme atonement sacrifice was finished and "your deal was sealed." One single offering completely cleansed and perfected, making us holy (set apart) now all that's needed is the acceptance of that sealed deal (*Ephesians 1:13*).

We, who have accepted God's grace, no longer have a sin problem! All our sins, He remembers no more (*Jeremiah 31:33-34*). God doesn't remember our lawless past, so why should we try to resurrect it and why waste valuable time rehashing old sinful memories. A memory is something that is not presently touchable. You can't legally be convicted of a crime where there is no solid evidence. Many have been sentenced to jail purely upon circumstantial able evidence, but heaven's court doesn't operate as ours. That should excite your spirit man!

In this agreement, set up from heaven to earth the Lord says, forgiveness of sins was accomplished. There is no longer any other need of an offering for sin. "I will put my laws in their hearts and will write them on their minds, and I will never again remember their sins and their lawless deeds" (*Hebrews 10:16-18*, emphasis added). By the power and virtue in His blood, we now have full freedom into the Holy of Holies. We can come and go as we please, initiated and dedicated by Christ. He opened up to us, a "brand new and living way," splitting the veil, which represents the separation from the law and grace, and allows us an audience before Him. We now have a personal one–to-one relationship, just another little nugget to consider.

Since we have such a great and wonderful High Priest who rules over the house of God, we are to press near with an honest and sincere conscience, with absolute conviction and assurance in His power. Our minds have been sprinkled and purified from a guilty evil conscience and washed with the pure water of His word. So hold onto your hope, which is the anchor of your will and emotions, without any double mindedness, without doubting your kingdom citizenship, confessing our allegiance, for He is forever faithful to His word.

All who considers the New Covenant as general and unsacred insults the Holy Spirit (*Exodus 24:8*), but you have been given great and glorious promises so, be alert, don't toss away your ability and willingness to secure what you have need of. There will come a time, when fiery trials come at you, not because of whom you are, but to whom you belong (*Mark 4:17*). You will need your confidence, so don't cast it away, be committed, unmovable, patient about performing and accomplishing the will of God.

You are forgiven; let's not forget that! Don't allow Satan to pull you away from that truth! By our faith joined together with His faith, you are to live by that faith. If we base our Christian walk entirely upon our works, we will end up boasting of our achievements, but if we acknowledge His work, then together, no other law applies to receiving His undeserved favors. The Lord has no pleasure in those who withdraw from faith, acting in distrust, for without faith it is impossible to please God (*Hebrews 11:6*). Just because He is displeased, doesn't mean He disowns.

His ways are faith's ways and not a way of withdrawal. When we have done all we can do within ourselves, we must stand our ground, maintain a good fight of faith, calling victories where victories cannot yet be seen. A good fight is a fight where you are the Victor, as someone once said, "To the Victor go the spoils." Who are these victorious believers? They are the ones who trust in, and rely upon God's grace. By allowing His faith to rise up and take control of and in every emotion.

We are told through His Word, "Stand still and see" the salvation of the LORD (Yahweh; Jehovah). Stand alert, watching God deliver and enjoy the inheritance among the saints (*Exodus 14: 13*).

Have you ever told a child to be still? I never made any money when offered as a little child to stand totally quiet; standing quietly takes a discipline that most children don't have. Being fidgety, over cautious, causing unnecessary movements, all are signs of having a double mindset and distracted of the situations around you. Not until serving in the U.S. Military did I fully understand the importance of being completely unmoving. If the enemy can't see your movement, he can't make a target of you.

We can see the apostle Peter being double minded in Matthew, Chapter 14, verse 30, "as he noticed the strong wind, he was frightened. As he began to sink, he shouted, "Lord, save me!" The wind had nothing to do with him walking upon the water, if not convinced, just try it on a calm day.

Being at rest in His ability, forgetting your abilities, and knowing God has your back, makes you the person in control; these are all signs of a mature soldier. I love this scripture in Isaiah 52:12 *"For you shall not go out with haste, nor go by flight: for the LORD will go before you; and the God of Israel will be your re-reward* (KJV emphasis added). Re-reward is defined as "Rearguard" (Strong Concordance); simply saying, "God has your back!"

Chapter Five

Do We Need Grace?

The tabernacle of Moses represented the spiritual path of a believer in the early Gospel Age, leaving the law, and entering God's grace. Entering the court through the door (Jesus) into the outer courtyard, as we walk, we can see Jesus as the spotless sacrifice on the brazen altar. From this point forward, only the designated priest can enter the first veil of consecration. Unfortunately, this is where many believers hang out their total Christian life, outside the blessings of Christ. They never come to the full knowledge of grace and totally accept Him as their Priestly gift.

In the book of Leviticus, we can see a description of the unrighteous bringing their offering before the priest for atonement. They were to bring the offering from the herd or from the flock. If the offering were a burnt offering, from the herd or flock, he would present a male without blemish. He would offer it at the door to the tent, laying both hands on the head, transferring symbolically, personal guilt to the animal while at the same time, reversing the innocence of the sacrifice to the man. The animal is then slain, its blood sprinkled by the priests before the Lord and upon the altar before the door to the tent.

Note: The unrighteous man brings the sacrifice before the priest and then, "he is no longer any point of interest."

Man's position in the atonement ceremony was providing the spotless, blemish free, sacrifice. The eyes of the priest now, are upon the clean, sinless sacrifice, not the sinful man! The man symbolically has exchanged authority of position. The man is "at present," after the transfer, spotless and clean, righteous, as the sacrifice was. The animal at that moment has become unholy as the man was;

symbolically transferring the sins of the man into the sacrifice of Christ. That's a pretty good trade don't you think?

This is why I make the statement, "God is blinded by the cross." He does not see you as an individual sinner. His focus is upon the sinless sacrifice! He views only the slain Lamb! Your unrighteous, sinful being, as in the historical Day of Atonement, is out of the picture; Christ personally took your sin, along with its despair, terror, sickness, and poverty. His own body upon the cross was as if He was on the altar. It pleased God to offer His only Son, Whom we might cease to exist to sin and live to righteousness in Him; by this relationship, we are whole.

After laying down our natural and accepting His supernatural, we, the believer, become as godlike as our Priest; as Christ became, for the priests of that day had a personal relationship and friendship with the High Priest.

We now journey through the holy place, feed upon the bread of truth at the Table of Showbread, become enlightened by God's truth from the Golden Candlestick, and offer prayers at the Altar of Incense.

Through the second veil, we experience His revelation of who He is. We receive deliverance through faith and by accepting the revelation of redemption, we become secure, not for a single year, but everlasting, eternal life. By the Holy Spirit now in us, we offer ourselves to the power of relationship in Christ.

The last section of the Tabernacle is where God lived, the renowned Ark of the Covenant. This is where He met with the High Priest and told of His wishes as, the Supreme LORD. The Ark of the Covenant, inside the last veil, is also a type of Christ, as was the Ark of Noah, a picture of deliverance and safety. Made of wood, it spoke of Jesus' humanity, with a layer of pure gold, which speaks of Jesus' divinity. Jesus was 100% man and 100% God. The weight of the Ark when traveling was about 1,500 pounds with the stone tablets, pot of manna, Aaron's rod, and all its coverings. It was the responsibility of the sons of Kohath (keh-hawth') to transport the Ark of the Lord, and the human body could not have handled such a task without the supernatural aid from God (*Numbers 4:4*).

The Mercy seat, also of pure gold, rested on the top of the Ark, as its lid. Beneath lay the representation of "past rebellion" from the children of Israel. All were under the Mercy Seat, out of sight, covered as in a coffin as dead to all, under the seal of Divinity, and "under the blood."

The High Priest would take the sacrificial blood of atonement and sprinkle it upon the Mercy Seat, signifying that everything "upon the Ark and in the Ark" was under the blood of the spotless lamb. All past, present, and any future rebellion, was covered. Some might have taken advantage of the sacrificial atonement and lived carelessly, barely walking a good path while others were upright and pleasing to God, but atonement at present offered the pardon for sins, regardless of their actions. The lamb was slain; blood was shed, sins now covered, all for a desired relationship between God and humanity.

Spotless Before God

Why do we need a Savior, why do we need a friend who is closer than our own individual family? We need His undeserved grace for we were created for a private communion with Him. We were created for closeness only His Spirit could provide.

Due to sinful pestilence brought into the world; all humanity was lost! We were doomed to an eternal hell. A hell prepared originally for Satan and his angelic followers, prepared as Satan's punishment at the time of his defeat in rebellion against God and His kingdom.

The prophet Isaiah states the world at one time, was all as ceremonially polluted lepers, all man's righteousness, "was" as a contaminated garment (*Isaiah 64:6*). The original meaning to the term "filthy rag" is, "a menstrual soiled garment," a garment used for female menstrual flow. Isaiah was saying any human deed toward God was filthy, polluted, and unclean. Our spiritual life is unclean by sin, dirty as a female sanitary napkin! In a sinful state of pollution, needing justification, for a crime, guilty only by association, we were eternally soiled. This filthy, unrighteousness is before the cross, not after! Now through the cross, by His blood, and resurrection, we are as pure as the sacrificial spotless Lamb.

Jesus is returning for people without any spot of sin, wrinkle free, and not even a slight blemish of a sin, however, no matter how hard we try; we will never be that clean! So, what are we to do? We don't have to do anything! Christ has done it all! This unworthy mind set has brought fear of rejection upon many whom eventually have given up, "back sliding" into their old lifestyle. Light has no relationship with darkness, but just because you are in a room with no light, doesn't mean that darkness is in you! Jesus said we were in the world, but not of the world. You are in an unworthy world, but because of your confession and heart belief, you are as worthy as Jesus Himself.

Paul tells us that this cleansing is not by any particular type of spiritual mumbo jumbo, dress code, hairstyle, church attendance, or tithing amount, which all are good, but are all physical works under the law. This cleansing took place long before you, or I became a believer in His gospel; while we were yet sinners, Christ cleansed us! We are consecrated before God because Christ is holy before God! Christ has given us the Father's righteousness through Him! He purified and made us free from sinful guilt, by a completed atonement. We were consecrated, set apart, and justified, at the time of His death pronounced righteous, simply by trusting the name of the Lord Jesus Christ. The effect of His death was the time of our life!

We, with Christ, spiritually hung on the cross and died with Him and resurrected with Him. Christ presently lives in us; and the state of living we now enjoy in our earthly body is a force of grace. Christ in us was our hope of glory. Christ is no longer a hope if we follow Him. A hope becomes a fact; a fact becomes secure; and we rejoice in that hope.

> *"For we were saved with this hope in mind, now hope that is seen is not really hope, for who hopes for what can be seen? If we hope for what we do not see, we eagerly wait for it with patience (Romans 8:24-25).*

We have been to the mountain and have seen the glory of the Lord. We, as did Moses, received His highest commendation, and walked away with His glory shinning not upon us, but within us. We have not only been to the mountain, but have looked into our future and crossed over our Jordan; we now are enjoying the promised land of rest.

Heaven Declares His Glory

The most damnable sacrilege that could be ever uttered is, "Humanity can earn God's favor by his or her good deeds."

Many believe there is some type of a god, the Man upstairs, Mr. Big, or a Creator, but fail to have a relationship with Him, choosing not to glorify the only true God.

People are most likely to express thoughts centered toward worthless things and display in ignorance their true nature. They claim to be wise, but often found foolish, they modify the glory of the incorruptible God into many images; trading the Word of God for lies, they applaud the actions of others over the works of the Holy Spirit. Even demons reverence His authority more than humans do, believing there is a God, and they tremble in His presence (*James 2:19*).

Even in today's world, as it was in Paul's time, people choose not to have a true acknowledgement of God, but obey their vain imaginations. Although they hear about God, they choose not to follow His voice, but agreeing with others who rebel boldly against Him.

Long before the creation of humanity, the heavens declared the glory of God; His birth through a virgin, His warfare upon Satan, His legacy toward the redemption for all humankind.

The three wise men from the east, traveled many miles following the glow of a single star into Bethlehem, which proves not only the ancient Hebrew were aware of the meaning of the constellation among the stars. The prophecy of Christ was foretold within the signs of the Zodiac and spoke of the glory of God years before the Law of Moses (*Genesis 1:14, Psalm 147:4, Job 9:9; 38:31-32*).

Abraham, the father of faith, must have known the signs from the heavens, for his ancestors, as well as his father, may have been moon-worshippers. The father of Abraham was "Terah" which is related with the Hebrew root word for the moon. Jewish tradition relates that Abraham's father worshiped many gods. This could be the reason he was to leave the religious pressures from his family, get out for his own advantage (*Genesis 12:1*).

Humanity needs the valid news of salvation because many religions spread only news of condemnation. Preaching a hope, "it will all be better in the sweet, by and by, is not a gospel of faith." The world needs the good news of a current salvation, "for there is now no condemnation to those who are in Christ" (*Romans 8:1*). There will be no need for hope in heaven.

Are you in Christ? Is Christ in you? If so, there is no judgment of sin lawfully upon you! No one can obtain the favor of God, or escape His wrath by self-works. No one except Christ can claim before God, or man, the fulfillment of the law, for within us, there is nothing good. Following the law to the letter was man's only salvation before the cross, but now, the law lives inside every believer. We don't serve God because of a rule, but we serve the ruler, under the Holy Spirit's direction. The believer doesn't keep the commandments finding favor with God, but the believer keeps the will of God because they have the favor of God.

All humanity, at one time or another has acted wrongly, omitting what they know to be right. Continuing in their plea for help, they failed to realize there is no help without Christ. Running from God, all memories of the gospel soon forgotten until their morality becomes questionable. Whatever hope is left is in their own ability to please God. All these actions show humanity has greatly dishonored Jesus' words of truth, and if spoken; it is with absurd superstitions, continuing wickedness, filled without of context opinions and half-truths.

As the light in the world, we should glow with confidence of whose we are, and in whom we move and have our being. Darkness represents the ignorance of a truth, and knowledge is emulating power. We become destructive for a lack of that power.

The light of heaven in the form of a man entered a world of spiritual ignorance. The world loved their ignorance more than the truth and rejected God's righteousness. Ignorance ruled their lives, but although their minds and their deeds were evil, God's favor, through Christ, super abounded and became their Victor.

Moses or Jesus

The Jews, as well as the Gentiles of Paul's day, did not like to hear any reminder of God's Word. They continued to commit deeds against their own reasoning as well as their personal welfare. Whether you are Sinner or Saint, you are predestined the same, but until you become knowledgeable in submission to Christ, you will never live out your destiny.

For those who desire to live within the law are ruled by its regulations, in which I may add, are impossible to keep. Please keep in mind, Jesus came and delivered you from the very law of regulations many are working so hard to keep.

Answer these questions within yourself; am I a New Testament believer? Is Christ my mentor? If so, why follow the prophet Moses instead of walking with the Messiah, Jesus? Moses disobeyed God, and this kept him from entering the Promised Land of rest (*Numbers 20:8-11*). Christ, on the other hand, fully obeyed His Father, thus entering the heavenly Holy of Holies, His eternal rest; sitting down at the righteous side of God, in a full rest. Oh yes, He seated us together with Him too (*Ephesians 2:6*).

Moses (law) vs. Christ (grace)

Under Moses, God demanded man to be righteous. *In Christ*, God imparts His righteousness unto us through His Son's finished work of the cross (*Romans 4:5-7*).

Under Moses, God visited man's sins down through the third and fourth generations. *In Christ*, God's grace never remembers our sins again (*Hebrews 8:12; 10:17*).

Under Moses, by perfect obedience to the Ten Commandments, man was favored. *In Christ*, we no longer are dependent upon our own efforts to receive God's grace because Jesus fulfilled the law on our behalf (*Colossians 2:14*).

Under Moses, disobedience to every commandment brought a curse upon humanity. *In Christ*, we enjoy God's favor because Christ became a curse for us (*Galatians 3:13*).

Under Moses, decent works produced a behavior modification without any heart transformation. *In Christ*, His finished work brings inner transformation, which produces excellent works that are motivated by God's love (*Two Corinthians 3:18*).

Under Moses, the blood sacrifices of animals covered man's sins for one year, and the process repeated every year (*Hebrews 10:3*). *In Christ*, *His* blood removed all sin…past, present, and future (*Hebrews 10:11-12*).

Under Moses, man's obedience could not produce any power to make them holy and just before God. *In Christ*, as we become conscious of His righteousness, we have the ability to overcome temptation apart from any self-works (*Romans 4:6*).

Under Moses, man continually sought for self-glory as he tried to obey the law, but always lacked confidence and could never perform well enough. *In Christ*, we have confidence and security because we are complete in Him, and He is the beginning and the end of our faith (*Colossians 2:10; 12:2*).

Under Moses, man had no relationship with God because of his unrighteousness. *In Christ*, we are righteous by faith and have a true relationship with God as our heavenly Father (*Two Corinthians 5:17; Romans 5:7-0; Hebrews 10:10*).

Under Moses, man could not enter God's presence in the holy of holies because he was unclean. Only the high priest could have an audience with God, and that was only once a year on the Day of Atonement. *In Christ*, we have the right to come boldly before the throne of Grace in any time of need because Jesus has become the perfect atonement for us (*Leviticus 16:2, 14,* Hebrews 4:16).

Under Moses, man was under a spiritual famine. *In Christ,* we are now under Jesus' abundant life (*Two Corinthians 3: 6-7, John 10:10*).

Under Moses, humanity was the children of God. *In Christ,* we all can now become the sons of God (*One John 3:1*).

Under Moses, the law provided the people a trainer, or guardian, but it was truly a type of guide to Christ.

The law was given to show humanity their need for God and lead them into holiness until the fullness of time for Christ was come.

The law was to justify and declare God's righteousness, to put humanity back to a right relationship, for without Him, all were unrighteous. All who were able live by its standards were found holy, but none were found holy, no, not one! Now through Christ, we are no need a trainer, or guardian (*Galatians 3:24-25*).

Christ has qualified us, making us fit and worthy as ministers of the New Covenant of salvation through Himself; not ministers of any legally written code, but of the Spirit. The Code of the Law kills, but the Holy Spirit gives life (*2 Corinthians 3:6*).

Jesus said *He* didn't come to destroy the law or the prophets, but to fulfill them (*Matthew 5:17*).

The voice of the law speaks, 'Do good get good, and do bad get bad." The voice of Grace says, "You get good because Christ did good." Improper English, but point made!

The scriptures say, you are doomed to eternal punishment if you do not live by the law, live and remain by all the precepts and commands written in the Book and practice them. The Law does not rest on faith; it does not require any faith; it has nothing to do with faith. The law relies entirely upon the actions of your flesh (*Galatians 3:10-12*).

If you depend upon any part to the law for your justification of sin, trying to obey its rules, or its regulations, you must keep the whole law. The law brings with it a curse, and if you fail any regulation, you fail in all, and are subject to its penalties. However, as Paul states, *"Certainly all who depend on the works of the law are under a curse. A curse is on everyone who doesn't obey everything that is written in the book of the law!"* (*Galatians 3:10*)

Regret vs. Repentance

We must understand that saying we are sorry to doesn't mean you have a repenting heart.

If you do a word study concerning the word "heart" of man, you find the "biblical heart of man" is not the physical blood-pumping organ that drives the directions of your body, nor the center that houses the Holy Spirit, but it is the center of your conscience.

Man is a spirit being who possesses a soul, and both live in your earth suit.

If you were to visit another planet, you would need a space suit. Your flesh is your space suit for earth. The heart is the center of the soul realm. The soul of man is your will, your purpose, your reason to actions, and the emotional center of our spirit being. Your spirit is the essence of who you are; you are created after the image and likeness of God, "the breath of God." You came from the inside of God and must worship Him in the same manner created, from the inside out.

You will live forever somewhere! Your spirit must have a place to reside. At physical death, your spirit and soul must leave their earth house because its dwelling is decayed. Gravity no longer has any hold upon your being. You will live forever in heaven or suffer Hell, not prepared for the saints. Your body and soul are the only parts that Satan tries to overpower, for they are still subject to the law of sin and death. Satan can't touch your recreated spirit; that's where the Spirit of Christ resides. Christ is not giving up residence, of what He has suffered and died for, shed His personal blood for; He's not vacating, not moving out! (*Genesis 1:26-27*)

Humanity is separate from any other creation of God, who is a distinct being, with a personality who thinks and reasons how to live out their days on this earth. We are able to reason with our Creator; He says we can come before Him and reason together (*Isaiah 1:18*).

The words "Image and likeness" do not mean that you are a cloned look-alike. Man is a created being, a representative of God on the earth with the same manner of rule. Man is to rule, have dominion; he is ordained and destined to be the King over the earth. Have you noticed Satan is a king wanting to be? He is portrayed as a Prince, and not a king? A prince is a king in waiting, but due to Adam's treason, his kingdom transferred to his nemesis, the Prince of the air.

Portrayed as a prince, he wants to be ruler, but has no domain. Without a domain, you can never rule as king, unless allowed by the powers presently in force. A Prince has no rule, no authority, and must adhere to the enthroned wishes. Adam's treason, gave the throne of earth's colony over to an unauthorized fallen angel.

Satan is an angel who, along with his host of followers, performed their own act of treason against God, then exiled to the earth. Never in line to become a king, is why he was outraged when God placed Adam upon earth, in a garden to be ruled by Divine workmanship; Adam was "up in the devil's business," ruling what Satan considered his.

A prince becomes as king when the current king is away from the kingdom; this is another reason Jesus needed to leave the earth, for He made the born-again believer's the kings and priests on this earth (*Revelations 1:6, 5:10*).

Created to be the original human king on the earth, Adam was to govern and rule, which included Satan, who was at that present time occupying the earth (*Isaiah 14:11-14*). Jesus said, He saw Satan fall like a flash of lightning from heaven (*Luke 10:18*).

Heart of a Matter

Man's heart directs his path with decisions that decide endless fellowship with God or unending separation in Hell; never-ending separation from God is Hell.

The blood pumping human organ that sustains our life while on earth is the English word "heart." In the Greek, the word for heart is "kardia." Pronounced kar-dee'-ah, the "heart," is, figuratively, the center thoughts or feelings from the mind; furthermore, by analogy, the middle (Strong Concordance).

The heart of humanity must have a change if desiring any relationship with their heavenly Father. The Apostle Paul writes in his letter to Rome, "If you declare with your mouth that Jesus is Lord, and believe in your heart that God raised him from the dead, you will be saved (*Romans 10:9 -10*).

We need to understand the reasoning behind the importance of our confession of faith, the importance in usage of our words. Confessing with our mouth is of vital importance to our relationship with God. We will normally repeat or speak what we believe is true, so let's speak our mind concerning our relationship with God's grace.

We should only acknowledge a trust in "the facts through the Resurrected Christ." We are acceptable before God, cleansed from all sin, past, present and future. Take a good look at the entire passage. Paul says we are set free from sin if we believe in our heart, and confess with our mouth.

Salvation is a two-part strategy set forth by God to secure our eternal destiny. Many teach the confession part of Paul's statement, but forget the heart, which also determines the deciding factor of your equation. One must make a heart decision with a voice declaration. We assume people automatically believe in their heart if they confess with their mouth, but not always true. We speak things we don't believe many times; it's called lying!

Many of us have heard the expression "talk is cheap."

Confession alone doesn't warrant any receipt for a debt paid. In addition, there must be a signature of trust. The "raised from the dead," portion of our welfare plan is a strategic factor. You must accept the gift of deliverance with your heart (mental assent), and then as an act of trust, in agreement, you proclaim its truth.

We need to emphasize the importance of what actually took place in the resurrection process, confirming our eternal security in Christ. We can mentally agree that God raised Jesus from the dead, but there is a deeper spiritual knowing, an inner "heart" revelation, which is activated by your measure of faith through the preaching on the gospel (*Romans 12:3; One Corinthians 2:4*).

If our faith is meaningless of divine truth, it is futile of divine effect, and becomes of no effect; just another imaginary religious fantasy (*One Corinthians 15:14*). If Christ has not risen from the dead, all Christianity is valueless! If He didn't forgive you of all sin, your salvation is vain! If He didn't make you complete in Him, His work at the cross is worthless!

Chapter Six

Repentance Brings Grace

Once you decide to study the scriptures, there is a personal responsibility in seeking God's grace. Some may try to live in God's grace by "mixing in" the Ten Commandments (law), but the Law of grace supersedes the Law of Moses and can't be mixed.

Purity is only in one or the other, not in both. When the Jews accepted the law, they were judged by every word; disobey one, be judged by all. On the other hand, if we accept God's grace through Jesus Christ, we are righteous through Him and not the Law. We obey the law because the law is in us, leading us to obedience. The totality of the law is in Christ, if we are in Him, then the Law is in us, in our inner heart. Complete and just, as if we, ourselves, have kept every word. We are not obedient to Him for acceptance, but because we are accepted, therefore, we obey.

Paul says, you are justified and in right standing with God through faith "only," and not by any work of any law. If you have absolute trust in Jesus Christ, in order to be free from sin, keeping any ritual is unacceptable. No human can ever be justified keeping rules or legal rituals, which are works by your sinful flesh. If you want to be righteous and in favor with God, you must walk the path, He has laid out for you (*Galatians 2:16*).

All Jewish children from a very early age are instructed to obey the Law of Moses, which refers specifically to the first five books of the Bible. These are known as the "Pentateuch," but can also refer to all Hebrew Scriptures beginning with the book of Leviticus. The Jews of Paul's day was unthankful and rebellious. They saw themselves as a holier people, entitled to particular privileges through obedience to the written law. All who acted in this manner, regardless of age, or race, were by their obedience of specific rules, judged. Every willful act of disobedience to God's grace is in contempt to His goodness.

To bring change to the unspiritual mind, there must first be a centered decision; a hatred of the former sinfulness, this is a true repentance.

Conversion is that great change producing a true repentance. The ruin of humanity is led by their un-remorseful conscience and to convert is to exchange the old for the new. The justice in keeping the law is the "full demand" of the law. One must continually keep its demands. Its demands are the motives toward a communion with its owner, which rejects all fleshly ambitions or motives.

Morally good people are those who have not received any teaching concerning the "Rituals of the Law," but perform good deeds by following their natural God-given sense of right or wrong. Those who demonstrate the good works within the law are following their internal conscience, accusing or even excusing them of any disobedience and become a law to their own self. If our inward conscience doesn't condemn us, we have not sinned. To whom must we answer? God is greater than our heart and therefore, our final judgment (*One John 3:20-2*).

In the description of unrighteousness, the principal fact of all humans will is their position of hostility against God. Those who did not have the written law had it within their sub-conscience at physical birth, which directs the influences of nature. Our inner conscience is our witness, and if acknowledged, first or last, good or evil; it will be our guide. As you keep or break natural laws, your consciences either will free you or condemn you. Nothing speaks more terror to the unbelieving mind (heart), or more comfort to the believing spirit, than Christ being the final Judge of all deeds committed.

Total obedience to the Law

Be aware that it is humanly impossible for anyone to keep the Law of Moses. Israel couldn't do it, so why do we think we can? Israel had to bring a spotless sacrifice before the Lord for their righteousness, and this is why we need, as believers, to observe and declare door number two. This door opens to God's grace, His undeserved favor by accepting Jesus Christ as your redeemer. We are to live by the law of faith in the power of His gospel (*Romans 3:27*).

Paul asked what if on one hand, you practice the law of circumcision and on the other hand, you would break its law, your work is counted as never being circumcised. Therefore, if an uncircumcised person keeps the Law isn't that the same as circumcision. They were not to judge a person's appearance outwardly; so neither was any works of circumcision to be openly judged. The circumcision of an inner conscience is the only true circumcision. Circumcision of the Spirit overrules the law of the flesh (*Deuteronomy 10:16; 30:6, Jeremiah 4:4; 9:25, Ezekiel 44:7*).

The law did allow the Jews an advantage for obtaining salvation under its rule. The stated ordinances, and the many favors shown to the children of Abraham, were all means of God's grace. The law was useful for the conversion of many, especially those that were completely faithful to it.

Unpopular to some, God's enjoyment is in the restfulness of His people; our happiness is His true enjoyment. His promises of grace are to believers only! Therefore, the unbelief has no promise of God's faithfulness. The door of salvation doesn't hinge upon our faithfulness, but upon His words and swings only in a forward direction. Opening upon a confession of faith and closing with our inner conscience, we accept His message of grace. Rewards, on the other hand, are according to our obedience of the faith in His Gospel, working His Word. A reward is a re-giving of a gift already belonging to you. The world sees a reward as an award for accomplishing a task, but we were in the ward-ship (dependency) of heaven since the creation. Since the sin of Adam, we lost our protection and positioning within the Supreme Court of heaven's judicial system.

The definition of "Ward" is a person (usually a child) placed under the care or guardianship of the state. The guardian, appointed by the court, is to care for and take responsibility for the protection of any future abuse or neglect: have custody, protect, safeguard with vigilance. The apostle Peter tells us that, through the full knowledge of Christ's divine power, we have everything we need for life and godliness (*Two Peter 1:3*). We are under Kingdom control, and Christ has restored our guardianship back to His authority.

Forgiveness of Sins

If we continue to dwell upon our past sin, it is because we have not fully become aware of our redemption heritage; no judgment to those who are in Christ. We must remember; Satan is our accuser, not judge! God is our judge, but not your accuser! When Jesus breathed His last faultless breath for your sinless freedom, were they not all cleansed up until the time accepted, your next week, and the following month and year too? Were they not cleansed for all peoples and all sins? God demonstrated his love for us by the fact of sending Christ to die for us before we sinned (*Romans 5:8; Revelation 12:10*)

What is the means to determine Satan placing condemnation upon you? How do you know if it is God's Spirit speaking to you? Ask yourself is the spirit I sense moving me closer toward God or moving me farther away from God?

All human flesh is under a burden of guilt, under Adam's transgression, enslaved to wickedness, a slave to its governmental dominion. There are several passages of scripture from the Old Testament, which describes the corrupt and depraved condition of mankind. Until redeemed by God's grace, we were all doomed! Our principles and morals proved irreverence for God and where no

Godly reverence lives, nothing good can exist.

Unlike fulfilling the law's demands, our salvation is not the result of what you or I can or cannot do for God. What Christ "has done" for all, no one can boast or take a personal glory. We are of God's individual design, recreated in Christ Jesus, born anew that we may produce pleasurable works. It was heaven's Planned Parenthood that prepared paths to lead us into the abundant life of Christ (*Ephesians 2:7-10*). It is only through our faith in God's grace, delivered from judgment and partakers of salvation. This is not our doing; it didn't come through our individual works, but it is a gift.

Since all fleshly works have a guilty residue, it is useless to seek justification by such works. Guilt is a dreadful word, but a law, which condemns for breaking it, can justify none. The sin principle at work in us stops any justification process.

King David made a statement in his writing that needs to be mentioned saying, "Blessed is the man whose transgression is forgiven, whose sin is covered. Blessed is the man to whom Jehovah does not charge iniquity, and in whose spirit, there is no guile. I confessed my sin, and my iniquity I had not hidden. I said, I will confess my transgression to Jehovah; and you forgave the iniquity of my sin" (*Psalm 32:1-6* Amplified).

Think about it, only the guilty ask for mercy. Mercy is giving a pardon in spite of a wrong committed. Only the unjust deserve judgment, but grace is the only mercy God shows. Grace covers a multitude of wrong (*One Peter 4:8*). Mercy is for the Sinner, but Justice belongs to the Saints. The righteous doesn't need God's mercy any longer, but they must declare His justice!

Spiritual Disease

Is there any cure for the spiritual cancer of sin, a disease plaguing humanity, eating away at our thoughts and keeping us under God's wrath? Grace is the only cure, and Jesus is the great physician that treated sin as a life stealing cancer.

Under the skilled practice of redemption, all cells are removed, the spirit washed and sanitized with purified water. The only rehabilitation is to enter His rest. Rest and relaxation are God's recommendation for our eternal souls. We are to cease from our labors, but at the same time, laboring to enter His peaceful rest (*Hebrews 4:11*). The only work we as a believer are to accomplish is to make an effort to rest.

The righteousness of His provision and His acceptance is open to His family of faith. This work of faith respects Christ as Savior, in all three anointed offices, as Prophet, Priest, and King. All are welcome into the family of God through Christ, by trusting Him, accepting Him, and holding to Him; every race, every creed. No difference, no race card allowed! His righteousness is upon all that believe; red, yellow, black or white, we are all set free by His might. Relationship restored, not only offered, but when accepted, righteousness placed as a robe upon them to parade as royalty. God's grace is free, and His mercy is everlasting, made new every morning! There is nothing within us to deserve such great favor; all blessings are undeserved.

Faith holds a special regard to the blood of Christ. It was the blood of Christ, which made the atonement; Jesus, by His own blood, declares you righteous, and you know that makes the devil mad! Grace comes freely for Christ bought it, paid for it, and allows us to cash in on its flow!

Sõde-zõ

Let's take a deeper look into the bounty of Romans, Chapter 10, and verse 9, which declares you will be pardoned if you acknowledge and confess with your mouth, that Jesus is Lord, and with your heart, believe, trust in, and rely on the truth that God raised Him from the dead.

Primarily, this Scripture is singled out as a Salvation passage, but opening the veil reveals more of God's light. If you believe and declare Christ's atonement, you will be saved from God's wrath. The Strong Concordance tells us that the word "saved" is an all-inclusive word meaning much more than our eternal security in Christ.

69 | Legacy of Grace

Salvation is not merely a get out of Hell-free card, but an all-inclusive style of divine living. The Greek word for saved is, sõde-zõ, meaning to: save, deliver or protect (literally or figuratively): heal, preserve, save self, do well, make whole. Let's look close at the three blessings of salvation:

> 1. Deliver is to bring, carry, distribute, convey, provide, present, supply, serve, hand over, relinquish, transfer, and give up.
>
> 2. Protect is to defend, guard, keep safe, look after, care for, and watch over.
>
> 3. Heal is to cure, make well, nurse back to health, restore to health, mend, repair, make good, reconcile, rebuild, and set right.

Were you aware of all these blessings? All are included in your confession of faith. As an old saying goes, that's a mouth full; remember you are a Ward of heaven. Christ is our Savior (guardian), the one who brings us these attributes of salvation. The Gospel of God is not prosperity, healing, peace, etc.; these are all inclusive in the Gospel message. The pure message of the Gospel is you have justification by faith through Jesus Christ. That's it, in a nutshell, what's inside the shell, precious food for nourishment?

Paul's message is simple, so simple it confounds those who profess great knowledge. Christ's badge of honor reads the original phrase, to Deliver, Protect and Serve! Therefore, our New Birth consists of much more than going to heaven when you die. We automatically receive this welfare package at the time of conversion, but how do we assure its benefits? The answer my friend is upon whom you depend. It is right there in His Word, if we trust without any doubt and speak its results, calling things, as God sees them, as though they exist, we shall have whatever we say! (*Hebrews 1 1:3*) Jesus said to have the God kind of faith. If you want to see the God kind of faith in action, read Mark, Chapter 11. As I have mentioned before, but is worth repeating; we are complete in Christ, and therefore, we have in our new recreated being, the God kind of faith; we just need to "realize it and declare it!"

The Relationship Blessing

What did the prophet Isaiah have to say in Chapter 5, verses 1-5, "He (Christ) has no royal, kingly pomp, that we should look at Him, and no beauty that we should desire Him? He was despised and rejected and forsaken by men, a Man of sorrows and pains, and acquainted with grief and sickness; and like one from whom men hide their faces. He was despised, and we did not appreciate His worth or have any esteem for Him. Surely, He has borne sicknesses, weaknesses, and distresses and carried our sorrows and pains of punishment, yet we ignorantly considered Him stricken, and afflicted by God, as if He had leprosy.

He was, wounded for our transgressions, bruised for our guilt and iniquities; the need to obtain peace and well being for us was upon Him and with the stripes that wounded Him, we "are healed, and made whole" (Amplified, emphasis added).

There is an unusual picture in verse five; because the word translated, "wounds" or "stripes" are in Modern Hebrew dictionaries with a different meaning. The word is "Havurah." The confusion comes because another root word is, "HVR," that relates to "Fellowship," so at least one Modern English translation used by Orthodox Jewish congregations in the U.S. relate the word "stripes" as "fellowship" and by having "fellowship with Him," we have our healing. We know we serve a God of relationships, and our relationship with Him is foundational to Godly living and to receive His blessings. Therefore, it makes sense that this study has much merit! Keep in mind that our relationship with Him is the sum of the gospel (*Isaiah 53:5*, One New Man Bible; Glossary, page 1741).

The Apostle Peter, speaking of Jesus, bore our sins in His Own body on the cross, so we, now being dead to sins, should live unto righteousness: by whose stripes, you were healed (*Chapter 2, verse 24*).

Peter speaks some very powerful words in his message of "being separated from sin; we should live unto righteousness, and because we have fellowship with Christ, we are healed. Isn't this what the act of communion is saying as we partake of Him symbolically? *(One Corinthians 11:24-31)* Paul says that some are sick and have died because they have not "fully understood the relationship of grace."

"As He is, so are we in this world" *(One John 4:17)*. Sickness is under the sin's curse, and Jesus bore our sin in His own body. Therefore, we are free from any curse due to the sinful state of man. The curse came because of disobedience in keeping the law. Peter said that we were dead to sin and are alive unto a right positioning, free from unrighteousness. Sickness and disease have only the right to plague the unrighteous lawbreaker; God has restored His righteousness to us the sons and daughters of His grace. God's word says, it rains on the just as well as the unjust, but grace has given us an advantage, whether we use it or not, we have an umbrella of faith. Furthermore, instructed through His word, we are not to think it strange when spiritual storms arise, so, when we sense a storm brewing, speak out your umbrella; have a sense to get out of the rain.

Our "confession of faith" is exactly that, "a confession of faith." How many times have you confessed Romans 10:9-10 without seeing or feeling any proof of your salvation? *(Ephesians 2:8)* Now, I have personally confessed my redemption without any heavenly feelings, other than my faith in God's Word, but I believe that I am safe eternally from Hell. To rely upon the senses to feel God's presence is foolishness, for your flesh will lie to you, but to rely upon His word that He will never leave you or forsake you, is godly wisdom.

I think about the reaction my own father had as I witnessed him going forward in a church service to accept Christ. I don't remember seeing a single tear, not one fleshly action except his confession to Christ. Many, including my mother, had little faith in his conversion due to the emotional teachings the church proclaimed, but his life was spiritually changed.

Curse, is a Curse.

A curse by any name is still a curse, and we must achieve any form of deliverance the very same way we received our salvation. The only knowledge of any redemption is "heart knowledge," the mental awareness that Jesus finished His purpose toward humanity, and walk accordingly. Let me coin a new phrase; instead of just saying, we are saved, let's declare we are.

sõde-zõed!

Go ahead, say it "I believe in my inner conscience that God raised Jesus from the dead. Through His death and resurrection, I believe I have been "sõde-zõed; delivered! I am being cared for, and have been restored to a right relationship."

That is powerful! Keep in mind; it is also the repetitive hearing of God's grace concerning healing that if allowed to take root that brings results. You will be like a fruit-bearing tree (*Mark Chapter 4*).

The muttering of God's word is as a gentle shower upon excellent soil and to grow a healthy spiritual tree watering is needed. God told Joshua if he wanted pleasant success, he must "speak (mutter: talk softly to oneself) His word continually, day and night" (*Joshua 1:8*).

Chapter Seven

Grace by Faith

The doctrine of justification by faith was very contrary to the philosophy the Jews learned from their youth. Therefore, Paul uses Abraham as his example, because the Jews boasted of their relationship to him, being of "his seed." His proclamation was justified in the identical manner as Abraham, and he was "justified by his faith." Not by his works! As a result, we today, who confess Christ, are justified by the same manor of faith. To stop any boasting, God designed the work of justification and salvation to come forth equally from His man Abraham. This doesn't make us lawless or irresponsible about authority, but resting upon the law of faith, for "faith also is a law" (*Romans 3:27*).

The rules of faith are simple in character. Confess your trust in what God says and be in relationship with His motives! Align your thoughts with His thoughts. See His grace an undeserved gift, and not as an act of your efforts, and you will possess what you declare! God's truth forms a relationship and makes a bond between you and heaven. As you agree of what He accomplished at the cross, you are "pardoned, and justified" by your faith within His faith. Unfortunately, the unbeliever, "remains" under sin's judgment

The law within itself, is still holy, revealing to us the past, and directing our future. Though the law as a covenant "cannot save us," we are to submit to it, as a rulebook into the hands of Christ. God has given all humanity the measure of faith to call upon Him, believing that He is, and He has accomplished our pardon of sin.

Paul warns us not to think of ourselves more highly than we should, not to allow our ego to get the better of us, and allow our opinions to overpower God's truth. God has given all the degree of faith necessary to come into the knowledge of His Son (*Romans*

12:3).

God gives us faith to accept His grace, and live His grace; mixing His faith with our faith gives us super abundant grace. We acquire our righteousness in the same manner as Abraham (*Romans 12:3*). Genesis, Chapter 15, and verse 6, reads, "Abram trusted in, relied on, and remained steadfast to the Lord. God counted it to Abraham as a right standing with Him" (Amplified).

Think about this; Abraham was a Gentile before he became a Jew. This made him "not only" the father of the Jews, but also the "spiritual father of all believers" (*Romans 3, 18-22; Galatians 3:6; James 2:23*).

Abraham wasn't circumcised until after proving himself before God (*Genesis 17: 9-11*). The Jews boasted of Abraham as their most renowned ancestor; however, exalted in various respects, he had nothing to boast about in the presence of God. Abraham was "righteous by grace," without any personal works, right only through faith.

Many years had passed before Abraham's failures added up, and his life was finished. Because of his obedience to his faith, they went forgivingly unnoticed. As stated in scripture, Abraham believed God, and that faith, added to him a righteous positioning (*Genesis 15:6*).

Lying twice to save his own life of his wife being his sister, Abraham still received God's grace rewarding him the prosperity of his enemies. Through the balance of his faith, he was paid righteousness, which purchased him certain rights with God. We also see from this example, if any man could possibly work the full measure required by the law, the reward would still calculate as a debt, which evidently was not the case of Abraham.

It clearly appears from the scripture, that Abraham was justified several years before his circumcision. It is plain this rite was not necessary in order for his justification; circumcision was an outward sign of corruption, of human nature, that needed to be cut away. The presence of the Holy Spirit is our New Covenant seal of circumcision, an "inward evidence" of righteousness by faith. Thus, assuring Abraham of being a partaker of God's righteousness by faith, God appointed the Jews to confirm His promises through his seed, and be

His known people. Therefore, we are to follow this example of obedient faith. Abraham is the spiritual ancestor of all believers.

The Promise through Faith

The promise of grace was long before the law. All spiritual families on the earth are in Abraham and the blessing points to Christ in reference to that promise (*Genesis 12:3*).

The law exposes God's wrath to all by showing that every transgressor is subject to its rules, but God in His mercy, has given us a promised blessing of an appointed faith, a faith "totally of grace and free of works." This faith makes sure that all are of like faith with Abraham, regardless of race, age, or education. Part of our pledge to His allegiance is justification and deliverance for all.

The nature and power of Abraham's faith were in full view, "he believed God," and anticipated the performance of His promise, even though his situation seemed hopeless.

It is a lack of revelation knowledge, causing us to plunge deeper into spiritual as well as physical depression and when confronted with difficulties, it leaves us wanting. Unbelief is the center of a staggering; double-mindedness, but Abraham did not waver or see his lack of a sacrifice being a point of argument or debate. God honored his work of faith, and paid him in righteousness for believing in His words. Pronounced faith honors God and God honors extreme faith. What makes our faith so great is allowing its evidence to be perfect in us!

Faith gives glory to God. Faith is our just tool by which we can receive the righteousness of God. We are justified only by our faith. Abraham's faith did not justify him by its own merit or value, but as giving him a right position in Christ.

The history of Abraham, and of his justification, was to teach generations, not to rely upon the merit of our own good deeds or actions, but upon Christ's true position with His Father. He is continually in the right position, and we are incessantly in His rest, together with and in Him.

Not by our merits did Christ's grant give us justice and salvation, but we were made whole together by His death and resurrection. He paid the debt that we could never pay by our own merits (Isaiah 53:8).

Now we are seated together with Him, far above and beyond any sinful circumstances (*Ephesians 2:6*). We have received a permanent discharge from any guilt or punishment of past, present, or future sins. This verse of scripture sums up the debt owed; all have sinned (past tense) and come short (past tense) of the glory of God, which I believe is Christ's death and resurrection (*Romans 3:23*). A right relationship before God is paid, as compensation, to all who believe and rely upon Him. By raising Jesus from the dead, He put to death our misdeeds thus securing our acquittal. The account against us is now absolved! All guilt before God is blotted out. He was both willing and able to save unconditionally and completely, and eternal. He is ever living to make the petition to God and intervene for us when necessary (*Hebrews 7:25*).

Christ is continually before the throne declaring our innocence, this is how we can have the confidence that we are saved eternally. "For it was pleasing to the Father whom the sum total of divine perfection, powers, and attributes should dwell in Christ permanently, and as He is, so are we in this world!" (*One John 2:1, 4:17* Amplified, emphasis added) God purposed that through the intervention of Jesus, all things would be completely reconciled (*Colossians 1:19 -20*).

Grace Produces Results

A supernatural change took place when you became a true believer in Christ; whatever is in your past, is past! You now are justified by faith, and have eternal peace with God through His blood. You are a new creature, someone who has never existed before (*Two Corinthians 5:17*). Justification takes away sin's guilt, and makes way for peace. Christ's peace passes all mental understandings, and keeps our hearts and minds at rest (*Philippians 4:7*).

Jesus is the great Peacemaker, the Mediator between God and man, so, let's be reminded that it is "His peace" He gives to us.

We were not physically born into this blissful state of grace, but re-born, born again, conceived by the very Spirit of God, and it is His Spirit leading us. We did not enter by our own merits, but we come as heavenly pardoned offenders. We stand boldly, not with bowed heads unable to see our Redeemer personally, but entering His presence with our head held high. We enter into a determination, and a boldness to obtain from His abundance: We stand firm and safe, upheld by the power of our faith.

Our carnal mind is not only an enemy to God, but also in the opposition to itself. Though disrespectable and unrepentant as we are, God's master plan is to deliver all humanity from sin's prison (*Romans 8:7; Colossians 1:21*).

God loathes the sin, "but not the sinner!" The sinner, on the other hand, loathes God and loves sin. Christ died, to bring a reconciled relationship. Wrath is God's punishment for all sin. This is determined by the absolute justice of God, and by His Divine grace. Get this into the depth of your being; God does not bring His wrath upon His righteous sons and daughters! As humanity believes in Christ and repents, they no longer fall within the power of sin and Satan's rule, therefore, are free from His anger.

By saving to the uttermost, the Lord has made us complete: This was the purpose of His undying love. When He said, "it is finished," do you think, He meant, "almost finished," "close to being finished," or as some from the southern states might say, "prêt-near finished?" NO! Jesus meant what He said. God says what He means! "IT IS FINISHED!"

Why do we as so-called Christians, talk and act as if it was not finished, not completed? If we believed it, we would say it, but most of all, we would act upon it!

We have a pledge of hope in our salvation and in the love of God through Christ. Even though tribulations arise, believers should rejoice in that finished hope, we can glory in God as our "unchangeable" trusting Friend.

Adam and Jesus

It exalts our views respecting the blessings Christ has obtained for us by comparing them with the evil, which followed upon the earth after the fall of our first fleshly father, Adam. Adam's nature became guilty and corrupt, and this guilt and wickedness passed down through his children, on to their children's children and then unto us.

All have sinned as the result of Adam and "come short" of the glorious plan of God's undeserved grace. Sin through Adam, covered the earth as a plague bringing with it physical as well as spiritual death. Misery entered through the curse of sin; and man died (separated from God). As the result of God's grace, man comes alive spiritually then lives eternally (*One Corinthians 15:44-49*).

The sentence passed upon all humanity was the sentence of death (separation of relationship); a sentence passed down as to a criminal. If Adam had not sinned, he would have not died spiritually and therefore, would not have died physically. Sin passed over the earth as an infectious disease that none could escape. In proof of our union with Adam, and our part in this transgression, sin prevailed for many ages before the giving of the law by Moses. Death reigned, not only over adults who willfully sinned, but also over multitudes of infants, which shows that all had fallen under Adam's condemnation, and that the sin of Adam, as cruel as it may seem, had been extended to all generations.

Adam was a picture of Christ, who was to come as the surety of a new covenant; restoring humanity back to relationship. Due to Adam's rebellion, all became out of relationship, but grace, and mercy brought back the gift of righteousness through the one Christ Jesus. Christ brought all believers into a safe haven, an exalted state from which man in Adam had fallen. This gift placed us in a state of justification, as Adam before he sinned.

Sin and death prevailed in condemning all, but by the righteousness of Jesus Christ, through faith, grace prevailed to the justification of all. Through God's undeserved favor, the gift of grace has increased unto many through Christ. However, many choose to remain under the dominion of sin. They followed their self-indulging emotions rather and receive the blessings of grace. This is heaven's good news; Christ will not cast away any who is willing to come to Him. We have much greater privileges than those lost by Adam; so by the righteousness of Christ, let us count our blessings.

The moral law showed the displeasing defects of humanity; tempers, words, and actions. Therefore, as shining a light into a dark room discovers dust and filth, which was always there, transgressions were also multiplied. The sin of Adam and its effects of corruption were a rebellion that appears over the entrance to the law. God's Holy Spirit reveals a most important truth: no matter how you may differ from another; every human is a rebel against God, and stands condemned by the law of their own actions; guilt by association, as they see themselves in His mirror.

We were all in need of a pardon. In a need of righteousness that restores divine relationships. There is no entrance or eternal reward without a pure and spotless righteousness. This purity cannot come from a mixture of sin and holiness, but only through the Spotless and Righteous Lamb.

The Love Reflection

The mirror speaks to us of a greater love, a love that shows stronger affection, a love that would give up his or her life for another *(John 15:13)*. The disciple, who knew firsthand, the meaning of this love, was John. The apostle John considered himself the beloved of God, and confessed as much throughout his gospel. In fact, he was the only disciple who fully understood how deep the love of Christ is in the heart of the believer *(Romans 5:5)*.

The apostle Paul tells us that this gracious love, by which all men will know that we are His disciples, is within our hearts at the New Birth conception *(John 13:35)*. "We have not received the spirit of bondage again to fear; however, we have received the spirit of adoption, whereby we cry, Father *(Romans 8:15)*. There is no fear in love *(1John 4:18)*.

The regulations within the law brought with it bondage and fear and no one could ever be satisfactorily, or holy enough. This brought great oppression; a distant fellowship and a suppressed relationship. God illustrated His love toward us, in that, while we were yet in sin, Christ died for us *(Romans 5:8)*.

We as humans could never perfectly love anyone or anything, for we are self-pleasing. The only love that gives all, and throws fear out of the window is Christ's complete (from the Father) love. How can anyone add to something that has no room for improvement? The love that drives out fear and brings us boldly before the throne, as a child to their father, this is Christ's perfect love, a boundless, never-ending love, a selfless love. This love works no wrong toward a fellow human. You can't get more flawless than perfect! Therefore, Gods love is the only thing that could fulfill God's law" (*Romans 13:10*). Where the Spirit of the Lord is, there is freedom, and liberation from sin's domination. If the same Spirit lives in you that's in Christ, you are as He is! (*Two Corinthians 3:17*)

Have you ever had the crazy idea that you were in control of your personal love growth? Christ's love edifies, constrains, has stability, supersedes knowledge, abounds, comforts, a bond of perfection, a spirit, covers a multitude of sins; it can be multiplied, and al-ways speaks the truth. We are to walk in this love, and grow in this love, but "His love" never grows! How will something that is super-naturally mature have room for growth? (*Romans 5:5, 13:10, one Corinthians 8:1 2, Corinthians 5:14, serves, Galatians 5:13, Ephesians 3:17; 3:19; 4:15; 5:2, Philippians 1:9; 2:1, Colossians 3:14, two Timothy 1:7, one Peter 4:8, Jude 1:2*)

Christ's love does not grow! We, on the other hand, are to grow "in His love." Every one of us has room for growth. No special works to perform, just allow the love of God to have its complete work in us. Through the Spirit of grace, I can at the moment love as Christ because I have His love within me. His love is now living within me; reaching out. Peter was instructed to forgive regardless of the offence, but human love can't accomplish this feat (*Matthew 18:21-22*).

Who is that person, or what is that place, or what is the thing, able to separate us from this love? Is it your boss, job, tribulations, distress, persecutions, an economy relapse, or maybe physical death can divide and conquer? I have searched the scriptures and must agree with the apostle John "nothing can separate us from the love of God!" Our love is in Christ Jesus! Our love is as He is perfect, and gives us boldness in the day of any Judgment. We will know when our love is mature; by the way, we react when faced with challenges. When Satan tries to bring judgment, our faith in Christ's faith, will stand its ground, not giving any place to the enemy. Before the foundation of the world, God has chosen us to be holy and without blame before Him. As He is, so are we in this world. He is love, and we are love *(One John 4:17; Romans 8:39; Ephesians 1:4).*

Chapter Eight

Dead to Sin, Alive to Grace

Without the New Birth, we are living outside of God's grace. Humanity does not have the Divine connection needed for a one on one relationship with God. This is why, to those living within the law, loving God with all your heart, soul, and body, is impossible to achieve.

The connection between justification and holiness is undividable, and the thought of continuing in sin and abounding in grace is inconceivable. True believers are lifeless to sin and therefore, not to follow its path. No one can be both deceased and alive at the same time. There is no such thing as godly zombies, only immaturity would think they could be separated from sin and yet live in it. You are as separate from sin, as you would be from a deceased friend or relative, memories are all that is left!

Water baptism signifies the act of dying to sin. Water baptism is an out-ward showing that you were buried and resurrected with Christ from all ungodliness and unholy pursuits, as well as rising up to walk with God in newness of life. Many profess Christ, but less proclaims His righteousness, which is the same. The reason is they have never mentally passed from death into life.

We are not to conform to this world's thinking, but change, by the renewing of our mind; think the thoughts of God (*Romans 12:2*). Because of great grandfather Adam, we have a corrupt nature, called the "old man," but a new life in Christ means the old life was crucified, dead and buried. All you have is stinking memories. Don't linger at the cross; Christ is no longer there! Don't hang around the tomb; Christ has risen!

Liberated from the reign of sin, we are now alive unto God with a lively hope free of any condemnation. This should entice every believer to be greatly concerned of how to conduct his or her selves before the world. Unholy lusts are common to the flesh, so let it be the mind of every believer, resist ungodly emotions. We all know it's inevitable; this physical life is soon to end, so let's encourage one another in His love. Distressful emotions cause us to sway as a young tree with every breath of wind, or stagger, as a person with too much wine, this will also cease in Christ. Let us be ready, fight the good fight in faith, for in Him; we are already over-comers by His blood, and using His words in our testimony (*Revelation 12:11*).

There is great strength in this covenant of grace. Sin has no more dominion over us! Can you sense the power in those words? God's promises to us are more powerful than our promises to Him. A true believer may struggle with sin, and deal with many troubles, but they have no dominion, no foothold. Sin will only aggravate, but never elevate to dominate.

Should any believer be so foolish to practice sin? These thoughts are repulsive and contrary to the Word of God. The whole design of God's gospel is for us to live under grace, not under sin. Is there a stronger motive against sin than the love of Christ? Shall we willfully transgress against so much goodness and love? Let us say, NEVER!

Slaves to Righteousness

Every slave is a servant to his or her own master and must yield to their commands. It is either the sinful disposition of his conscience that leads to physical actions, or the new and spiritual obedience. There are two ways of viewing sin; before Christ, one is dominated by an alien power, both struggling for victory. Another sees a loyal servant of God, once the slave to sin, but now a recreated child of God. Sinners can't help but practice sinning! Believers, on the other hand, may often miss their mark, but never counted out of the game!

Shame came to the world carried on the back of sin, and we all can see its effects; sin birth's death. More distressful than physical death was the spiritual separation from God. King David said God's loving kindness was better than life itself. The ways of sin may seem pleasant and inviting for a season, but its road leads to death.

The believer, on the other hand, is free from sin, and has total liberty; for where the Spirit of the Lord is, there is liberty. If the fruit of grace is unto holiness, and if there is an active principle of true and growing grace, the end is surely everlasting life; a very happy ending! Though the way may seem all up-hill, or the road too rough to walk, His grace is still sufficient. Though you walk through a valley, He lifts you up as with wings like an eagle, and gives you strength. Christ has given to us this precious gift; He created it, then prepares us for it, and next, preserves us in it *(Two Corinthians 3:17)*.

Marriage and the Law

As long as an individual continues using the law as their covenant, seeking personal justification by obedience to such law, they remain slaves to sin...Nothing but the Spirit of life in Christ Jesus can make you free from the law of sin and death. Accepting Christ and His righteousness, brings you under a brand-New Covenant.

Believers are liberated from the power under the law, which condemns sin. We are released from that power, which stirs up and provokes lusts that dwell in our fleshly nature. The law of sin demotes us to an animal type, selfishness, ruled by nature's senses

No longer are you under a covenant of works, the gospel of Christ, supersedes the Law of Moses. The difference spoken by Paul is as being married to a new husband. Our second marriage is to Christ. By death, we are released from any obligation to the first, as the law of Moses states, a wife is released from her vows at the husband's death, therefore, our faith makes us dead to the law, and has no more power for we now have a "brand new master," and our new master rules with undeserved favor. Adultery is having an affair with a second partner while married to your spouse. Have you ever thought that mixing law with grace was committing spiritual adultery? With passionate love, our works are the fruit of our union. As fruit grows from the vine and is the product of an "oneness to its root" we also should bear fruit, but until one belongs to the Vine, there can be no fruit from the branches, no union, no fruit, therefore, no food given throughout the world. Jesus said He was the vine, and we are its branches *(John 15:5)*.

A vine yields all its nourishment to its branches, whether large or small and the nourishment of each branch and stem passes through the main stalk that springs from the earth. Therefore, Jesus is the root of all real strength and grace to us. He is our leader and teacher, and through His Holy Spirit, imparts grace and strength to us, as we need. Our fruit is our witness. Many have thought their witness was to pass out salvation materials, testify to their co-workers, and place religious pictures or opinions upon Internet media. Although all these methods may be useful, we are to be a witness of His loving grace into our lives first. He takes care of all the branches of His vineyard.

There are many whom by words, say they are branches yet do not show any fruit. Do they really belong to Christ, if so, where is their fruit? We can see leaves moving in the hot air of their words, but no substance. Some may appear as branches, using vocal professions, but bear no inward heart possession. They are as dry tumbling weeds, unacquainted with a personal relationship with Christ as their Redeemer, unfruitful professors of Christ and no more. Every branch that "bears no fruit," is an injustice to the rest on the branches, and taken out of the way, so the "true branches" can grow.

A branch that bears no fruit, is not attached to the vine, if any person is in Christ, he is a brand-new creature altogether and the old previous immoral condition has passed away, and a fresh and unused life has evolved! (*Two Corinthians 5:17*) Jesus said, some professing to be His, will stand before Him and boast of their good deeds, but He will proclaim that "He never" knew them (*Matthew 7:23*). I do believe He was speaking of deceitful prophets and of course, the word "false," tells us the heart of His story.

Indwelling Sin

Except you were to live and follow the fullness of the law, there was no way to become exempt from your sin. The law shows no mercy or grace for you are guilty of all if you fail one rule. The apostle Paul said, he would not have known his sinful thoughts, motives, and actions, except through the law. The law was that perfect standard that showed how wrong his life and thoughts were, proving his sins more numerous than he had imagined. The law as designed was to show only the weakness of spiritual character, not to keep any from failing.

Paul, once a Pharisee, found himself with difficulty seeing his individual inward wickedness. Needing correction upon his character, ignorant of the spirituality of the law, he felt like a criminal when judged. Seeing what the law demanded, his own sinful mind kept him from fulfilling its obligations.

The law "is and forever will be sacred." The unholy sin principle is still very much alive in our human nature and produces rebellious emotions. The law was issued to uncover the central emotions of our conciseness revealing our need for a relationship with our creator. There is nothing too good that a corrupt and vicious nature will not try to pervert.

The identical heat that softens wax will also harden clay. The duplicate fire that burns the flesh will as well keep it from freezing. Food or medicine when taken wrong may cause death, though its nature is to nourish or to heal. The law, by the same example, may cause spiritual separation through man's wickedness, but sin is the poison that brings this separation. It is not the law, but the "sin discovered by the law" that brings spiritual death. The damaging nature caused by sin along with our human conscience now hangs in plain view.

Compared with God's holy rule of conduct within the law Paul gives us hope. He found himself very short of perfection, and seemed to be as a man who, against his will, sold into slavery to a hated master from whom he could not be free.

A true believer "unwillingly" serves this hated master, but cannot shake off the annoying chain that holds down any chance of rescue. The only powerful effort strong enough to break its chain is the love of Christ! The law, although directed by God was made from the earth, written upon stones and troubles the flesh in service to God. God's grace, on the other hand, is Christ Himself, from the Father to you, written not upon earthen materials, but upon the heart of every believer. The law can't overcome your spirit, but your spirit in grace overcomes the law!

The apostle Paul teaches, although we desire to do well we sometimes fail for sin is always present, rising up through our flesh. We yield to be evil, even though it is against our fixed determination of will. The motions of sin within us hinder, and by our flesh fighting against His Spirit, we can't perform as the Holy Spirit directs. In addition, in opposition of the Spirit, we can't do what the flesh wants us to do either.

The "believer," according to our inward new man, is "under grace." Our will directs us to holiness, delighting in the law of God, and in the holiness it demands. How different this is from those who make themselves an easy target with regard to their internal emotions. Their flesh prompts them to do evil and even with warnings from their inner conscience, go on against the grace of God and practice ungodly things.

Paul sometimes felt unhappy and heartbroken thinking, where would his release come from? How would he free himself from the chains of death? Then he realized God was his deliverer, not him! He would receive his deliverance through Jesus the Christ. With all his will and emotions, he served the law of God, but with his flesh, he served the law of sin.

Grace Never Condemns

God never condemns those in Christ, for through faith; we are secure by our own union with Him. Any judgment brought before you, although inspired by Satan, is all "human" reasons.

What is the principle of our faith walk, the flesh or the Spirit, the old nature or the new, corruption or is it grace? Which of these do we make provision for, and govern us? The unrighteous is unable to keep any commandment of the law fully, for it requires an inward obedience, not outward duties.

The Holy Spirit has written the law of love upon the minds of humanity, even though His righteous law has not become as one yet. His love is complete in the true believer, who answers only to the intention behind the law. The favor of God, the welfare of your soul, and the concerns for eternity belong to the Holy Spirit, and those who seek Him will find Him, and receive of His Spirit. Which thoughts, may I ask, bring your mind the most pleasure? Which thoughts motivate your morals?

Christ in You

Are you intelligent to God's kingdom or more aware the world's desires? By the power of divine grace, the world can be subject to the law of God, but their sensual minds never can be. Their lustful mind needs to be changed first. This is what repentance is all about. We must have 180-degree turn in our thought patterns, a complete turn from the will of Satan to the will of God. We are instructed to live in harmony and be of the identical mind and purpose of Christ; having His "never changing love." Allow His attitude and purpose to be our example in humility, being in full accord and of one harmonious mind (*Philippians 2:2, 2:5; Titus 5:9*).

If Christ lives in you, because of His righteousness, your spirit is very much in relationship with God the Father. However, because of sin, the natural body is separated from God. On the other hand, if the same Holy Spirit which raised Jesus from the dead dwells in you, He can restore a new life to your mortal short-lived body. So then, you are not duty-bound to your carnal nature set up by the dictates of the flesh. You are not to live by its standards, but according to the dictates of His Holy Spirit. We will genuinely live eternally with Christ if we refuse to be dictated by the flesh and trust in His grace (*Romans 8:10-13*).

Paul tells us although a child may be under age, and an heir to an estate, they are no different from a servant. Although they may be the master of an estate, they remain under administrators until the date fixed by their father. Those Jews also were as minors, and like slaves under the rules of the Ten Commandments. They were liable to its rituals, and to the observations and teachings.

We are no longer servants! We are free to come and go as we please by the grace of God, and are called "sons" and if sons, then, "we are His heirs." The Spirit of Christ's dwelling in you is His Holy Spirit dwelling in you! Christ Himself said, pray to the Father using His name. Unfortunately, some still pray to Jesus, and wonder why He doesn't answer (*Galatians 4:1-7, John 16:23*).

Grace covers all! Our will, reason, and emotions, our new nature is His nature. We are alive to God, and the righteousness of Christ assigned to us secures the soul from spiritual death. Therefore, we should understand why it is our duty to walk focused upon His grace, and not our senses.

If we live a lifestyle according to our five physical senses, we will certainly become separated because of their lusts, whether we profess Christ or not. It is "not only with our confession" that Christ dwells, but "believing" within our inner-conscience. Let us, by the Spirit, make it our goal to cast down the fleshly desires that exalt over the will of God. Restoration by the Holy Spirit brings a new and divine life to our will and our emotions.

The people of God, by His Spirit, have the temperament of children. We do not have a spirit of bondage, as the Old Testament church did. We own the spirit of adoption and no longer walk in darkness as an outsider of that early dispensation. Adopted children are set apart from rejection and should act as care-free members, but an orphaned child lives under an unwanted fear of rejection.

Sin has been, and will always be the cause of all suffering that exists between God's creations. By receiving Christ, our desires are accelerated; our hopes are encouraged, and life's expectations are raised to higher heights. Our weaknesses may seem many and great, overpowered and showing no hope, but the Holy Spirit will always over shadow and empower us.

Predestination

Nothing that earth can offer is equal to God's free grace! The gift of His Son was sent to be the atonement for our sin, and our union with Him is incomparable. He has given us all things that affect our life and His godliness. He has prepared for us, a crown and a kingdom. He has supplied our every need according to His riches in glory by Christ Jesus.

The Holy Spirit teaches us what to pray for and how to pray. As a sanctifying Spirit, as a comforting Spirit, He silences our fears, and helps us overcome our many discouragements. The Holy Spirit knows the mind and will of God, and encourages us as He searches our renewed mind. The enemy cannot succeed in their plans of destruction because the Holy Spirit makes intervention to God on our behalf.

To the image of Christ, we were predested. Think about it, even though we deserved destruction, Gods determined to restore us by regeneration through the power of His grace. Called unto holiness, the gospel is His purpose, and any who once was enemies, now. He calls to come home. Those he calls, He justifies, but only those who accept His calling are justified. Those who He justifies, He also glorifies. Those who dare stand against His call still abide under guilt and wrath.

If Christ justifies us, who has the authority to condemn us? However, how are we justified, by what power are we secure? By our merits or the merits of His death are we saved? His death for sure, for His resurrection was and is the total convincing evidence of divine justice. Paying our debt with His blood and conquering its grave was Christ's greatest victory.

Whatever trial may attempt to separate the believer; this one thing is for sure; nothing can take Christ from the believer, and nothing can move the believer away from Christ. Be confident, for His love secures you! I ask again, who or what is powerful enough to separate us from God? You can be evicted from your home or separated from your loved ones, but nothing can separate you from the love of Christ; what authority! Isn't that powerful!

Everything held most valuable in this life can't compare to the peace that those few words give your soul. To those who do not know Christ, the only thing left which they would gladly part with is the condemning guilt of all their sins!

Does Christ revoke His love for those who fail to keep mortal requirements? Is His salvation plan hung upon the hinges of humane efforts? Missing the mark is not forfeiting the game! If His love is in us, and nothing can separate us from that love, well, you know the rest of the story!

Chapter Nine

The Need for Grace

Whatever God does must be just! God's grace alone makes us unlike any other: holy, sanctified people. No one can or has ever deserved it. We, who are His, must be thankful to Him only. God has obligated Himself only to act by His promises; His revealed will. Who are we to judge the Divine counsel of God? Would you not allow the infinite God the identical self-governing right to manage His affairs, such as an inventor or a potter may exercise over their creation? The potter makes every vessel from the same lump of material, but each different from the other. Does this appear as unjust? If God can do no wrong, His management of the players in His plan for humanity is divinely inspired, acting as He wished to make way for His Son to redeem the world. He formed vessels from the earth, and filled them with His Spirit in preparation for His glory.

Sinners, not God, shape themselves in their own hands for hell, but it is God, who has formed the saints for heaven. The fault exists in the hardened sinner himself. God hates sin because it is an insult to His holy integrity and character. We should respect His mercy and creative abilities, and make every effort to secure our position in His Son.

Our Future

Luke records, as was Jesus' custom, He entered into a synagogue. He began to read from the book of the prophet Isaiah, "The Spirit of the Lord Jehovah is on me because Jehovah has anointed me to preach the Gospel to the poor. He has sent Me to bind up the broken-hearted, to pronounce liberty to the captives, and the opening of the prison to those who are bound, to proclaim the acceptable year of Jehovah, and to comfort all who mourn" (*Luke 4: 16*).

As He finished reading, the eyes of the people were focused attentively on Him. He rolled up the scroll, and sat down. "Today," He said, "this Scripture that I just read has been fulfilled while you were listening" (*Luke 4: 21*).

Jesus quoted from verse 2 of Isaiah Chapter 61, but left out the last sentence which reads, "And the day of vengeance of our God." If He had read that sentence, He would have fulfilled that verse too, and we would not be enjoying God's grace as we are today. Jesus said, this scripture has now been fulfilled while you're listening" (*Luke 4: 21*).

Some may believe God predestined His creation to an unending heaven and others to an endless Hell, but if this were true, would He not be an unjust God? In His preparation for His glory to prevail, God positioned His creation to play out the role that would justify His eternal plan. He is a creator with a holy purpose, and the glory of the cross was His extreme end to all ungodliness. He purposely fashioned and strategically positioned His creation in the dispensation of time to carry out His will; therefore, we must keep in mind that there are two sides to God's eternal purpose. There is the law and there is grace, both have distinct tactics of operation, and different endings, but the same purpose (*Ephesians 1:10*).

Paul had a great desire for Israel's salvation, but the Jews sought after a righteousness of their own rather than God's plan. All humanity must hear the gospel of grace and believe it's the good news for every race, color, or creed; His righteousness by our faith.

The Jews based their eternity upon a foundation of human works, and refused Christ legacy as their gift of salvation. Today many religions do the very same in various ways.

The strictness of the law showed the need of salvation, but they were blind to the ceremonial meanings of the law showing Christ as fulfilling all righteousness, bearing the penalty of the law on the cross. Even those that were under the law were justified before God and obtained righteousness by faith. Because of the cross, all are partakers of His perfect righteousness.

Christ has fulfilled the entire law by paying all of humanity's debt for transgression. Therefore, whoever believes in Him is justified before God, as though they had fulfilled the whole law person-ally.

Keep in mind; if there were no Judaism and no law, there would be no Christianity.

You can separate Judaism from Christianity, but you can't separate Christianity from Judaism. Christianity is born of Judaism.

Is the law opposed to the promises of God? If a law could award spiritual life, righteousness would have come by the Law. If the law, engraved in stone, made the Israelites unable to look upon the face of Moses because of its brilliance, shouldn't also the privilege of the Holy Spirit cause men to obtain and govern with greater glory through Christ? (*Galatians 3:21, Two Corinthians 3:7*)

Justification by faith in Christ is open before the mind of every person and left to no excuse or doubt. If you "confess" you're faith in Jesus, as Lord your and Savior, and really "believe" in your inner-conscience that God has raised Him from the dead, you become the righteousness of Christ through faith by the power of the Holy Spirit. There is no faith justified, which is not powerful in sanctifying man's conscience, and regulating all its affections by the love of Christ. We must devote and give God our minds and our bodies; this is our reasonable service. Our minds do the believing, and our bodies do the confessing. "May the God of peace himself made you holy in every way, so that your whole being, spirit, soul, and body, be kept blameless at the coming of our Lord Jesus Christ" (One *Thessalonians 5:23*).

The Confession of Sins

For those who worship God with a works mentality instead of a divine revelation of grace by the Holy Spirit, might ask, "If we don't confess our sins how we will keep our relationship?

How many times have we heard a good brother or sister giving honor to their unbelief by "proudly declaring," and I quote, "Just an ole sinner saved by grace?" Now don't get upset, but I ask you, how can you be an ole unrighteous sinner, if washed in the blood of the

Lamb? Please think about it! You either are righteous (saved) or sinner (unrighteous), you can't be both!

Allow me to ask this question; have you confessed all your sins today, all your worries, fears, or all those ungodly thoughts? Have you confessed all your doubts? If you have, you are a better person than most! None has confessed totally all! The apostle Paul teaches, whatever is not of faith, is sin. According to his statement, any form of unbelief is sin! Have you doubted today? Let me say again, the law has no room for faith; the law is based upon works only and breeds a self-righteousness attitude. There are religions that live by personal works to help secure a favor with God by the length of their hair, dress, facial hair, color of their clothes, and much more religious nonsense. They are not living by faith, and therefore, all their self-efforts still equal sin. Have you confessed that self-righteousness sin? (Romans 14:23)

If you make forgiveness of sins an individual responsibility, you must make sure, you confess 100%, all the time, or you will be guilty of every sin. Now, if you feel the need to confess your sins, before a man or before God, to be righteous, you must confess every point of sinning every time. If you don't, you are guilty for them all. Judgment shows no mercy! Remember, the nation of Israel was obligated for atonement every year, but that one time lasted the total year. Jesus is now present day atonement under Grace, lasting eternally! Jesus said, His yoke was easy and His burden light (James 2:10, Matthew 11:30).

Would Romans, Chapter 10, verses 9-10, apply to the sinner alone and One John, Chapter 1, and verse 9, read for the believer? Should we divide the two apart from each other? If you review the context in which John is writing, you will see he wasn't addressing the believer in his first letter, but in fact, the unbeliever. John's gospel must be in agreement with the Apostle Paul, wouldn't you think, and in agreement with Christ's teaching also, otherwise, it wouldn't be a harmonious gospel. In the book of Hebrews, Chapter 8, and verse 12, in which Paul speaks on behalf of God states, "I will be merciful to their unrighteousness, and their sins and their iniquities will I remember no more." Ask yourself this question; Am I right with God because I confessed all my sins, or is it because I accepted the supreme sacrifice of my Lord and Savior, Jesus Christ? I trust you chose the latter!

You must accept Christ's forgiveness for "all your sins," past, present, and future. Not by your faith in your dress code or good deeds, but by your faith in His finished work of the cross. You cannot have both! Don't mix law with God's grace; it is as oil with water, and again equal to spiritual adultery.

To proclaim personal works to receive divine favor is teaching a rewarded position in Christ by pure law. Do works of the law save you, or are you safe by His work of grace within the Law? Any real New Covenant relationship with God is between God and His Son, not upon human efforts! Now, I will admit; this gospel of grace sounds too easy and good to be true for our feeble minds to grasp, but God didn't want to make it difficult, just finished, complete, and eternal! (*Romans Chapter 3*)

Do you think Jesus might have had dementia? He was only thirty three when he died? You think. He might have forgotten to tell Paul about the necessity of man confessing their sins before Him. He laid out His last will and testament on the road to Damascus before Paul without mentioning the confessional doctrine. Alternatively, maybe it was Paul, who had the memory loss, forgetting to include this doctrine in his letters to all churches. I'm not trying to be funny, but Paul makes it very clear, "all our sins are forgiven" according to the riches of God's grace, and "not by any fleshly works of man's efforts!"

If Paul never preached or taught any doctrine based upon a personal confession to receive salvation, one would think he at no time any such doctrine to keep it either. Confession of individual sins is a doctrine based upon the law of good works. I can understand why Paul received much opposition from the Jews in his day, coming against the law of works. I can name several today, whom acting in the same manner as the Jews, are against Paul's message and refuse to accept the gospel as free of works. Some become irate when speaking against those who practice confession before a physical priest of certain religions, but preach confession of sin before God. Jesus as our High Priest never included this doctrine within His New Covenant.

You might ask, but what about one John, Chapter 1, and verse 9? Doesn't it plainly state the confession of sins? Okay, yes it does, but when one looks closer, you will see; (1) to whom John was addressing his letter, (2) what did he actually say, and (3) what were the circumstances of such a statement? Please remember, when we interpret God's text "out of con-text," we normally end up being "conned!" Let's "rightly divide" His word and not be conned into "mixing the law with grace."

The believer will have no cause to repent of his sinful past before the Lord ever again, for "we were previously justified and acquitted; for all, acquitted before the highest Supreme Court in or outside the universe."

Gnosticism

Throughout Paul's writings, you will see a common thread of greeting to the churches. He directs his speech "To the saints," "to the church," "to the sanctified," or "to the called." In the introduction letter to the Hebrews, he wrote the highest of all revelations to the Jews and reminds them that the Son of God sits enthroned at God's righteous side. John's first letter also depicts a certain group of readers. In Chapter 1, verse 1, there is no greeting to the believer. He does, however; greet the believer directly in his other two letters. He writes in Two John 1, "The elder of the chosen lady and her children, and not only I, but all those who know the truth," and in Three John 1, he writes, "the elder to the esteemed Gaius, whom I love in truth," but there is no greeting to the believer in one John 1.

In his first letter, John was addressing, a serious infiltration of heretics who entered the church known as "Gnostics," which did not believe in any existence of sin. John is saying, in verses 8-10, if you say, "you don't have any sin; you are deceiving yourselves, and God's truth is not in you!" If you say, "you have sin, Christ is faithful and righteous, and will forgive your sins and cleanse you from all your unrighteousness." If you say, "you have no sin, you make Him a liar and His Word is not in you!"

The term "Gnosticism" does not appear in ancient sources, but is history, and first coined by Henry More in a commentary on the seven letters from the book of Revelation, where he used the term to describe the heresy in Thyatira. Plato as well as Socrates was role models of Gnostics in the Roman era. The usual meaning of the term "Gnostic" is "learned intellectual knowledge."

A common characteristic was to teach a "mental assent" as the way to salvation. The Gnostic idea of God was "a compassionate creator of the universe who works to make the universe as generous as limitations of matter will allow."

Some identified Jesus as, "an embodiment of a crowning being who became incarnate to bring insightful knowledge to the earth while others totally denied Christ as any supreme being, but merely a human which had attained divinity through a "special knowledge" and taught His disciples the same. All this information is available on the Internet.

First John 1:9-10

First John, Chapter 1, verses 9 and 10, is, clearly to the unbelieving Gnostics. Written to encourage the truth and "stop their infiltration of denial of any existence of sin." Paul tells us that all "have" sinned (past tense) and come short of God's glory, (the cross)" so we need to accept the fact of sin as a curse, and we must accept Christ's forgiveness of all sin. To accept the cross, is to accept, once for all, "cleansed of all unrighteousness." This is why in Chapter 1, verse 1, John writes, "The One Who was from the beginning (Christ) Whom we have heard, seen with our eyes, looked upon and touched with our hands concerning the very word of Life, you also can have (future tense) fellowship with Him and with us" (Amplified, emphasis added).

Paul's letter to the Romans, Chapter 10, and verse 9, is also in harmony with John's letter with a prayer reference, all should pray in acceptance to Christ as personal Lord and Savior. How often do you need to repeat the prayer of salvation? Should we start every day with a prayer of salvation? Paul didn't say if you confess with your mouth "repeatedly," but a one-time confession, with a long-time possession!

You don't become born-again, and then re-born, once more, and again! In the same manner, how often are you to confess your sins for forgiveness and cleansing when you had nothing to do with the new birth experience to begin with? Paul never asks us to confess our sins! He does say to confess, "God raised Christ from the dead and confess that He is your Lord." We are to "repent" (acknowledge Christ's death, burial, and resurrection toward our lives)! One would think Paul would have added confession of sins in his proclamation if it were truly a doctrine. Remember, Paul didn't read about his gospel from the religious text, but personally received the gospel from Jesus Himself. Think of it in this manner; just as a child reacts to a loving father when corrected, we also respond in love as our renewed mind brings to our attention all our unrighteous ways. We are to repent, turn 180 degrees in our thinking, birthing works of faith, promoting God's grace.

Our Elder Brother, our Advocate, our Lawyer is seated at the Judge's side and reminds any accusation of the nail-pierced hands, thorn-pierced brow, and pierced side, as "the receipt" of payment made for the debt owed. Our sins also were nailed to the cross with Him, buried and resurrected to walk in "newness of life." If our "heart" (inner-conscience) does not judge us "we have not sinned!" As His blood flowed, our righteousness glowed, light in a darkened world (*Romans 6:4*).

We were not physically born within the kingdom of God, but adopted (re-born) into the royal family. To become a citizen, you must pledge your allegiance to the Kingdom of Heaven. The Holy Spirit introduces you to Christ; together they present you before the throne (by the authority of Jesus' name). You must decree your allegiance in the presence of all the host of heaven! You accept His legacy as you agree with the Christ's atonement for all your inherited sins. You speak boldly before all that Christ is your Lord, and your adoption into the Family of God is complete. You are accepted and placed in right position with God's kingdom; The Father regards you as equal to His first-born Son.

To continue your life on earth and in preparation for your eternal kingdom life, you now have all things that pertain to life and godliness. All this takes place in Romans, Chapter 10, verses, and 9-10.

The Holy Spirit

Jesus speaks to His disciples of sending His Holy Spirit after His departure, and the Spirit's position within the world. He said He speaks a truth; it was for their advantage that He left them, for if He didn't go, their "Helper" would not come. Now, when His Spirit comes He said, He will sentence the world of sin, righteousness, and judgment; of sin, because they do not believe in me; of righteousness, because I am going to the Father, and you will no longer see me; and of judgment, because the ruler over this world has been judged" (*John 16:7-11*).

Jesus said He was speaking a truth, so we need to listen to that truth. The ministry of the Holy Spirit is three fold: (1) judge "the world" of their sin because Christ is not Lord (2) "correct their thinking" on righteousness, because He would no longer be in their midst as their righteousness, (3) and "change their thoughts" on judgment, because Satan is already judged.

Paul says he shared with Christ in His crucifixion. It was no longer he who lived, but Christ! The life he now portrays, he rules by faith, and reliance on a complete trust in the Son of God, Who gave Himself for him. He no longer treats God's gracious gift as a minor importance, defeating its very purpose. If a righteous justification and the acquittal from guilt come through observing the ritual of the law, His death had no meaning, and Christ died for no purpose! (Galatians 2: 20-21).

The law was a mirror reflecting the unworthiness and ungodliness of humanity! Although the people murmured and complained (sinned) multiple times, God kept them warm at night for 40 years, cool in the heat of the day, and fed them bread from heaven, and supplied fresh water miraculously from a rock. He clothed them, and their shoes lasted for 40 years!

The law was to reveal their need for God and not self-righteousness. They declared through their own self-efforts to accomplish anything God commanded! Their initial act of rebellion was breaking the first commandment given; making a graven image of gold and worshiping it (Exodus 24:3).

As the word of God also is a mirror today, The Holy Spirit, uses the Word, revealing who and what, but most importantly, who we are in Christ. We can't blame the mirror, as we look forward to capturing our true image, "What we see is what we get!" The mirror is to behold our reflection, not the pre-conceived idea of our thoughts. It is not a physician to heal the abnormalities it reflects! If the mirror reflects a blemish on your face, you can't rub the mirror on the blemish and make it disappear! You must properly apply the correct means for its healing. Paul said he would not have known sin unless the mirror (law) revealed it to him, but he could not use the law to remove the impurity, for God's grace is the only ointment, the balm of Gilead (*Jeremiah 8:22*).

As we allow, His Holy Spirit gives us a true revelation as we look into His Word. We will truly see, In Christ, "Who is the fairest of them all?" We look on the outward, but Christ lives on the inward spirit. We must continue by faith and rest in what God sees in us!

After our New Birth, we are in the world, but no longer of the world. Christ is our Lord (owner)! Unless I am misreading the verse, and I'm open to the Spirit to correct, the Holy Spirit only convicts "the world of not accepting Christ as the Messiah," not those already in the family. We have no need to be convicted (sentenced) for sin, for we are clean of all unrighteousness. Due to the power of the cross, we now have God's personal righteousness, no need of judgment, for there isn't any condemnation to those in Christ. Satan has already received judgment, separated from God, and eternally sentenced.

So then, who convicts us of missing the mark? It is our "heart," our renewed mind. "Beloved (believer), if our hearts do not condemn (convict) us, we have confidence (righteousness) in the "presence of God." We have learned that our heart is our inner renewed conscience (*One John 3:21*).

Is There a License to Sin?

Reading in another chapter, John addresses the believer by saying, "little children, because of His name," your sins "have been" forgiven.

Salvation is the result of Jesus' name, not of any human rituals or personal confessions! Is John speaking confusion concerning our eternity? I think not! We as believers need to be less sin conscious and more righteous conscience if we desire a more blessed life. (*One John 2:12*).

One day, the religious leaders asked Jesus a question, testing Him of which commandment was the most important of the law? Some commandments, they said, were easier to follow than others. Jesus replied saying; the first commandment is the most important, love the Lord your God with "all your heart" and "all your soul" and with "all your intellect." The second is in comparison; love your neighbor "as you do yourself." These two commandments are the sum of your righteousness before God. All the Law and the Prophets depend upon these two. We must keep in mind; the law was the salvation of the Jew. Our salvation, on the other hand, is within the confines of the law of faith in Christ's name not rituals of dependency. (*Deuteronomy 6:5; Leviticus 19:18; Matthew 22:37-40*).

Have you ever given much thought to how you were to accomplish these two great laws? We read like, well; this is just what everyone must do, but have you met anyone who has ever accomplished these laws? I haven't!

The most important word is "all" your heart soul, and mind. Without God's personal love, humanity was a failure looking for a place to succeed. Obedience to the commandments of God's law, was His Love; not only fulfilling the law, but the completion of the law. Without God, we cannot love with our whole of anything! Humanity is incapable of loving unconditionally! Our earthly love is consistent with "What will I get in return." Here resides the good news of grace, the gospel, "God's love, and is poured out "in our hearts" (inner-conscience) through the Holy Spirit,"
This takes place at our acceptance of Him (*Romans 5:5*).

Jesus fulfilled the law concerning us loving the Father, by putting His Spirit within us at our New Birth. It is no longer a law to love God with all your heart, soul, and your mind, but loving Him is at the moment the brand new you. In your heart, soul, and mind, you have a fresh desire. Now that is good news no matter what religion thinks!

We cheapen the grace of the cross by thinking that His suffering for our forgiveness is only good up to the point of our acceptance. We must then be dependent upon our personal work of confession to make heaven. God did not save you on the installment plan! He paid your debt in full, not one sin at a time. A true believer "will no longer practice sin," but will look to the cross, the beginning and the end of our new faith. We learn to comply with its results and go boldly before God for help in any time of need.

Righteousness in the Old Testament was to "do right" before God, but in our New Contract with heaven, it is to "be right" before Him; a verb requiring action by the subject of the verb. When we are righteous by our faith, the Holy Spirit leads us to change our behavior; the outside showing of what's on the inside. We are His righteousness, "the justified" of God in Christ. Not "our righteousness," but it is "God's own righteousness," imputed to us. If our actions fail to change, it is because we do not truly know Him (Romans 3:25).

In the mind of the Jew the word, "believe" requires a change in one's behavior.

God's righteousness and holiness are the foundation of any believer's lifestyle. The only way any person can acquire holiness, as God, is to receive "God's personal Holiness" which is Jesus the Christ. You will want to do right because God's nature to do well with others is now inside you.

As far as the east is from the west,

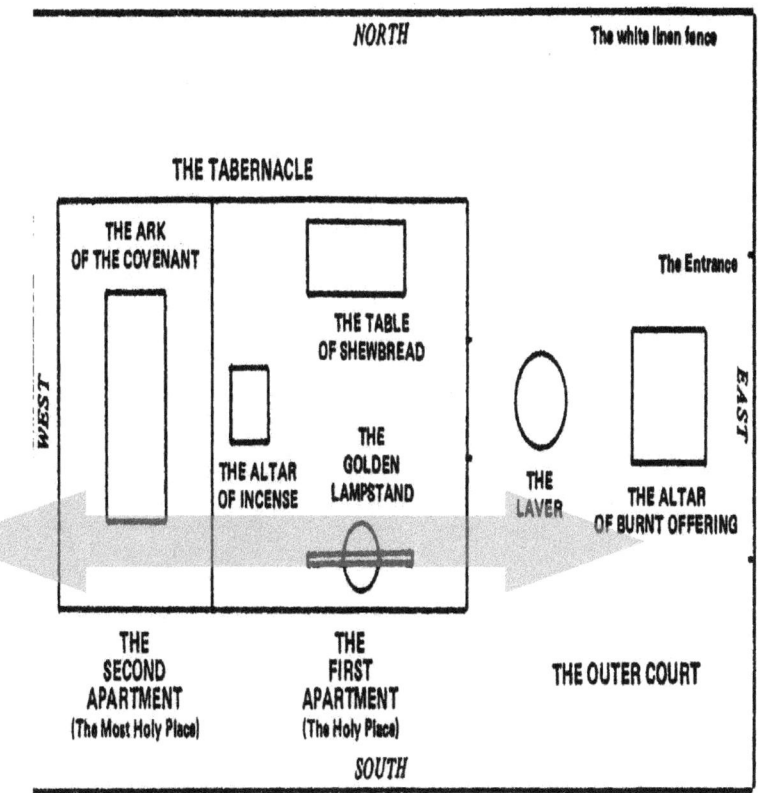

He has removed our transgressions!

Chapter Ten

Falling from Grace?

I trust that you have read the previous chapters before looking into the controversial ending to this book? The religious church has argued this question from the time Paul laid the foundation to the Roman Church even until our present. Can a believer fall from grace? Since you are now here let's continue to experience God's eternal love upon humanity and search out what His word has to say of this subject.

We, as believers in Christ, who are redeemed, are free from the penalties of the law through faith in Jesus' finished work. If we choose to neglect this great legacy of God's grace, we will fall back under the curse of that law.

We rob ourselves of the joy, and full blessing that Christ purchased with His own blood by returning to a system that operates under impossible regulations. These laws of "do right, be blessed, do wrong be cursed" is no longer valid to the believer. If this law was righteous, would Jesus have needed to die, shed His blood to pay our debt?

If the works of the law did not save us and make us hallowed, why do we think those same works will keep us spiritual? Just take a moment and think about it.

I remember giving my life to Christ at the youthful age of 13. As a teenage boy, I heard the preacher preach about fire and brimstone, a burning hell waiting for lost souls! I accepted Christ purely out of a fear of burning forever and ever. A ticket into heaven and the escape from hell was what I wanted. My spiritual upbringing was, don't cuss, drink, or smoke. Don't have sex out of marriage, and hope to God you are good enough for Him to answer your prayers. Whatever you do, don't do anything to make Him mad. This may not be the exact message, but that's what I heard.

I wandered away by the time I had reached 16; thinking serving God was too hard of a life to follow. My friend, if I was taught what I am telling you now within these pages, I would have saved myself much heartache; righteousness through the strength of Christ's redeeming grace.

My salvation, as a young teenager, was purely an emotional up and down roller coaster experience. I repented countless times, said I was sorry for my sins, even cried scores of tears, but was not stable for the days that lay ahead. I had the presumption that when I was doing right, God was happy, and I would feel Him, but when pressure at school was high and the "feeling" of God's presence was low, back to the old nature I went. I thought God had left me many, many times. I would go to Sunday school and church, feeling close to God, but return to a miserable next six days.

Let me interject this thought of "feeling God" for a moment. I acquired an emotional religion. Over looking any devotion, I became a servant to my emotions. A "feels God" religion; I accepted the fact of never being able to live what I thought was a God pleasing. I did what many unlearned newborn believers do; I gave up! I rebelled and stayed out of God's way until coming to my senses in my early twenties.

I was tagged a "backslider" on my way to Hell, so I just accepted their prognosis and off, I went.

As I look back upon my early life, I realize something was different. Before I accepted Christ, I at no time gave thought about sinning, it never crossed my mind. Now I was ruined for sinning! A still small voice was trying to lead me, guide me, and direct my ways; only if I had listened. God was now speaking to me all the time, ruining what I thought was a fun lifestyle. I didn't recall Him ever speaking to me before. He was gently showing me I was playing in Satan's toy box and needed to change.

While in the U.S. Army, serving in Vietnam, not knowing if I was to return home in a body bag or walk from a plane, God kept talking to me. I wish I could have said talking with me, but at the time, I figured He was mad at me and didn't want anything to do with me; a worthless sinner.

I would not have considered myself "a bad sinner," although I don't know if there is such a thing as a good sinner. Some of those things I was told would send me to hell, I was doing. Subconsciously, I figured since I was on my way, I might as well enjoy it! The point I want to make is, as I have reviewed my experience many times, I know that God never left me! His Holy Spirit spoke up from the inside me, wooing me gently, trying to help detour my direction. God wanted me blessed, but I was in rebellion against His directions.

If God had left, why was He still bugging me, correcting my thoughts, messing with my head? Satan would have taken over if he could have, but the Holy Spirit of God Himself had sealed me, just as He does every born-again believer.

You should be thankful God doesn't leave or disown you because of your spiritual immaturity!

He said, "I will never leave you! I will not at any time forsake you!" I don't know any other way to say it that would explain it any better. If Satan can get you to doubt God's grace, you will not communicate with Him.

I daily walked through a valley of death, and its shadow was heavy all around me, especially through my term in Vietnam. I wasn't talking to God except before I would fall asleep, in hopes I would not die from a rocket or mortar round. I would do what I wanted during the day, then pray and ask God to forgive me and not forget me during the night when we might be attacked with enemy fire; waking the next day to continue a "selfish life." I am so thankful God overlooked my dumb spiritual adolescence and had the love and patience to lead me back into His domain.

I am so grateful that God's grace never left! He was strong in my weakness, but I never realized it. His grace was more than sufficient to keep me safe! He was always speaking, but I was so spiritually immature that I couldn't distinguish the voices. His "sheep" know His voice, but I was an infant lamb in a big human body. I never took the time to become acquainted with His voice. An infant learns the voice of the parent by an ongoing relationship, a communication that builds a trust.

The Holy Spirit would not have spoken to me if He wasn't inside trying to lead me along a path of righteousness, but I thought, why talk to someone who wasn't there? Only mentally unstable people do that.

Falling Back

Yes, my friend, yes a believer can "fall from grace," for I fell from His favors, but falling from grace is not losing your birthrights! If you depend upon "your own ethical works and not on God's righteous grace, you will surely "backslide." God may use your emotions to reconnect with you, but He teaches to never be a servant to those emotions. You will "fall back" into your old self-righteous living condition.

I failed because of thinking I could never keep His commandments, and you know what, I was right! I know now; I didn't have to, and neither will you, for "Jesus is keeping them for us." In Him we are complete! Our part is only to trust Him. We must confess, and allow Him to do the rest! All Ten of the Commandments are fulfilled in Christ, and we are in Him! The Jews worshiped by their emotions this is why it was so difficult to accept Paul's message.

A sinner has no conviction to do right or any remorse over doing wrong; there is no light in sin's darkness. This is how one earns the name, sinner. Sinner's sin because it's his or her lifestyle. A believer, on the other hand, may act unrighteous due to a lack of communion, which leads to a lack of trust in God. Lack of knowledge leads to a failure to understand one's positioning in Christ; it misses the bull's eye of our high calling in Christ.

Paul spoke to the Galatians who relied upon legal rules for their righteousness. He said, they have "separated themselves from Christ" and "fallen away from grace" (*Galatians 5:4*). That's what I unknowingly did; I separated myself from His grace (favor) and became a rebellious child. I thought His wishes were too hard to follow, and if He really loved me, He wouldn't make serving Him so difficult! Falling from Grace: According to Paul, must be the "falling back or the returning into self-works" and Returning to rules and regulations, trying to govern our lives within a failed system.

God's laws didn't fail humanity; humanity failed God's laws.

I used to think falling from grace was falling back into sin, thus separating oneself from God's protection, but how can we who are lifeless to sin, fall back into a "non-existent" state. How can we live to something that is promised to be "deceased and buried?" Once you start depending upon your "own self-righteousness" to secure your salvation, you fall away (backslide) from God's undeserved favor.

Paul declared, as many as followed the laws were under its penalties. They were cursed in those things, which have been written in the scroll of the Torah (teaching). Please realize that it is not God who penalizes you when you miss His mark, but it is the law itself that condemns! It is "impossible" for humanity to live by a law that brings condemnation and death with it. If you fail to keep one statute, you are guilty of breaking all. In essence, the law that can save you will also kill you. None is righteous in God by following rules; the only law that you are to live by as a believer is, "the law of faith, not a law of unattainable rules" (*Deuteronomy 27:26, Galatians, 3:9-14*).

The Ten Commandments (the Do Not's) has nothing to do with faith (Can Do's). Whatever the flesh sees, feels, hears, tastes, or smells; the five physical senses rule. The one who follows these senses must totally live by the means of them. To be mentally free from the law, you must declare, "Christ "has" redeemed me from the penalties of the law. If someone asks you, "When did you become liberated from the curse of sin" you should boldly respond, "When Jesus took my place on the cross, but I just heard about it and believed it on such a date" (*Leviticus 18:5*).

Christ says you "were redeemed" (past tense) from the curse, and the blessing of Abraham "is upon all who come Him." We have the promise of the Spirit through faith. If you recall, the blessed promise of Abraham was "RIGHTEOUSNESS BY FAITH through His Holy Spirit" (*Deuteronomy 21:23, Galatians 3:14*).

God does not say, we are cursed, when we fail Him; He says we are "redeemed from the curse!" Jesus died to redeem us from the curse of the law, for "without the law there would be no knowledge of sin." We as believers fall under the curse "when we fall back under the law" and try by "our works," to uphold its statutes. Therefore, when you miss the mark, "the law" condemns you, "not God!" Forgiven is past tense.

Missing the Mark

Through Christ, we have hope when we fail, and "we will fail!" Although through the power of redemption, we fail less each day for as someone once said, practice makes perfect, or in this case, righteous.

The curse of the law keeps you from the blessing of Abraham, not the curse of sin! Sin is breaking the law, but where there is no law, there are no lawbreakers. The curse is its only penalty, and Christ has "taken our sin," so we no longer are sentenced to a spiritual separation. Sin is no more a problem to the believer; our problem is our insistence on living under ran an earthly system to become holy, which depends upon self-works. I'm going to repeat that again, a believer's problem is the insistence on living under a system, which depends upon self-works to keep a relationship with God.

One must agree those who sin deserve its judgment, but Christ has taken our sin and freed us from its penalties. Where does this leave you as the believer? That leaves us released from the law of sin and death, unattached from its judgments, but righteous under His grace.

God credits righteousness to us apart from any self-works!" "King David says, "to be envied are those whose sins are forgiven and covered, covered and buried (as dead). Blessed and happy; envied are those whose sin the Lord will take no count against." David lived under the law, but had a revelation of what God's plan was for the earth (*Psalm 32:1-2, Romans 4:7-8* Amplified).

The Greek word for our English word "sin" means: "a failing to hit the mark." That's simple enough to understand, every time you sin, you fail Gods will; plainly "missing what you were aiming for." If you were target shooting, and you missed the bull's eye, you sinned against the will of the game. No one took away your gun and bullets. No one took your bow with its arrows when you failed to hit the center target. You may have failed the moment, but never the game;

you lay aside your disappointment and prepare for another time. You take another opportunity, try, try, and try until you hit the mark.

With God, it's no different; you keep on trying, and trying, and trying; soon you realize you are hitting more and more, and missing less and less. The Apostle Peter calls this, "growing in grace" and the apostle Paul says it like this, "I press towards the mark for the prize of the high calling of God in Christ."(*Philippians 3:1; Two Peter 3:18*; KJV).

I propose these questions; have you ever missed the will of God? That one was too easy. Now, turn off your religious mind. Can you miss the will of God, remain saved and still go to heaven?

If your birth name was Johnson, but your adopted name was Smith, and were in front of a firing squad when told all with the name of Johnson, would be shot; would you fear for your life? No, you would feel relief for your old name had no acquaintance with your new one. You would rejoice because your past was dead to you. You would declare to all that could hear, I'm safe; I once was a Johnson, but now I'm a Smith. You have been adopted and given a new name, a name that will be forever recorded in the census of heaven.

If we are doomed because we fail God's purpose for our life, we may just as well stop now, hang it up, for as long as you are in your earth suit you will continually fail God; this is why Jesus came to set you free!

While in an earthly body, we miss the mark of our high calling every minute of every day, in fact, if you say you don't, John says, the truth is not in you! So then, What is this mark that we are to aim and hit? Is it to feed the poor, give to charities and be more kindly to our fellow man, or is there a mush higher calling?

Sin is not missing God's righteousness, for in Him; we are righteous; right with God all times, you are whom "God says" you are! We must read the Kingdom Handbook (Bible) and learn what He has to say about His family. The kingdom handbook states, our righteousness is apart from the law of sin and death, and a redeemed person (believer) stands righteous before the Lord eternally. Separated from the law of sin and death, makes us in "right position." King David said, let the redeemed of the Lord say so. Well, what are you waiting for? Are you redeemed? Then SAY SO! (Psalm 107:2)

Ready, Aim, Shoot

Jesus told those under the law, to seek His kingdom target "first." His kingdom and His righteousness must have been His number-one priority. Before you accepted Christ, the Ten Commandments were your guides to favor with God, but after Christ, the Holy Spirit is your guide. This must be the mark of our high calling in Christ "His dominion and right positioning." After we seek, we find, after we find, we accept, after we accept, we walk out His domain; no need to seek any longer. The woman, who found her lost coin, rejoiced and declared her victory. The one, who lost his little lamb, also rejoiced and declared his victory. No need to search for something that isn't lost! *(Matthew 6: 25-33)*

What humanity lost was their kingdom positioning, their rightful place within God's kingdom. Christ's kingly domain is His relationship with His Father and in Him; we can move freely and have our being.

His will is for none to perish, but all to have "everlasting life." As the words of a simple song say, "Be happy, don't worry!" Don't speak your fearful thoughts! Enter "His rest," be restful; be anxious for nothing and you will not sin. You are finished, complete, and eternally free within the realm of His kingdom.

I have always related worry as to, spending time is a rocking chair; just something that occupies your time, but never takes you anywhere.

Let's read Romans, Chapter 4, and verses 6-8 (Amplified) again, but this time, let's use the Greek definition placement of the word for sin "missing the mark."

Blessed are the lawless ones who have **missed the mark**, they have been forgiven, and those who **miss the mark**, will be covered: blessed is a person for whom the Lord would not count **missing the mark** against them (Emphasis added).

The Lord Himself said He would not count "missing the mark" against us. I don't know about you, but that excites me! This representation brings a brighter light upon any dark areas of confusion concerning the sins of the flesh. Our flesh is still under the curse because it is of the earth. The rebellion of Adam fell upon the whole earth, and everything connected with it. Our fleshly body will decay, but we will receive a new one. Sin can't enter heaven, so, Jesus took care of your sin problem; your spirit now can enter heaven, but without its earthly body; this is why we will receive a brand-new body, a body not subject to the earth's sinful state. Our unused body is not for occupying heaven, but the new earth (*Revelations 21:1-24; 22:1-5*).

Let's take a look at what the apostle John had to say, "No one that is born of God practice's sin! Why? God's seed abides in him! Indeed, he cannot go on sinning, because he has been born from God. This is how God's children and the devil's children are distinguished. No person who fails to practice righteousness and to love his brother is from God. This is the message that you have heard from the beginning: We should love one another. We know that the person who has been born from God does not go on sinning. We know that we are from God and that the whole world lies under the control of the enemy. We also know that Jesus has given us understanding so that we may know the true God. We are in union with his Son Jesus Christ. He is the true God and eternal life (*One John 3:9-11; 5:18-20*, emphasis added).

As a person in Christ, we are not to work any self-achieved righteousness of our own workings; based on any physical earnings to the Demands of the Written Law. No position derived from a ritualistic worship, can possess the genuine righteousness through faith in Christ. (Philippians 3:9).

Therefore, it is not our confession of sin that keeps us in a harmonious relationship with God, but it is the act of stopping lifeless works, which in their actions bear no fruit to righteousness! We fail God by our lack of faith in His finished work on the cross; for this is the "Legacy of Grace."

The Gospel is not a system of notions, but a life of practice. The beginning progress of a strong faith; not only heard, but also believed is its only work. Those, who have received a revelation of God's grace, are most likely to feel imperfect and their own weakness viewed the most. There is not only His supernatural counsel, but also an abundance of heavenly riches, which are precious and valuable. God's divine counsel is complete in us! There is such a vast distance between God and man, between the Creator and His creature, which only His grace can bridge (Ephesians 3:18)

New Life in Christ

As we transform out of sin's darkness into His marvelous light, Divine Grace moves us closer toward our destiny. Loving others with pure hearts and returning good for evil should be our goal. The grace of God teaches us, in general, to live "godly, alert, and righteously" and to deny all that is contrary to the matters of the cross.

Paul makes a powerful appeal by asking us to surrender our bodies as a lively sacrifice, submit all we are, all we have, and all we can do unto Christ. This is our only acceptable surrender, our duty to "walk and live" in the Atonement of the spotless Christ lamb.

Our continuance of a renewing work of grace is in progress. Sanctification is our living to righteousness more and more, by missing the mark less and less. The great enemy to this renewal is mental conformity so be careful not to trust in carnal things when making plans for future happiness, they soon will pass away. Don't fall in with the customs of those who walk in the lusts of the world for their thought's center only upon earthly matters. Genuine repentance is the work of the Holy Spirit, which first begins with an "understanding heart." Changing into the likeness of God is the knowledge of His righteousness, and pure holiness in you. To be godly is to surrender and rest within God's grace.

It should deeply sadden us knowing the power we have and yet failing to use that power. Since the time of Adam, humanity has become enemies to God and to one another. In a world whose smiles seldom agree with God's grace, those that embrace their salvation must expect to meet with its adversaries daily. The line of our function is clearly marked out. We are not to seek any personal vengeance. Your enemies will be judged and sentenced by the wrath of God and when strife and revenge are on the attack, those that forgive are the true conquerors.

Evil for evil is an animalistic compensation, suitable only to the animal world. Animals have souls; they have feelings of emotion; they can think, but they can't reason. Animals are ruled by their senses; therefore, no reasoning ability and no consciousness of any being above them, or of any existence hereafter. Animals have no conscience of right or wrong. We, who are higher than the animal kingdom, should study the things that make for peace. This is a hard lesson for a dishonest nature to learn; a remedy against this nature is not to give place to wrath! When passion is up, and the temper strong, give it time to dismiss, but be aware, both will return. What separates us from the animal kingdom is the power to reason, our emotions.

The believer is as unarmed and naked as Adam and Eve in the garden after their rebellion. Your armor is vital to secure your soul from Satan's temptations, and assaults of this present evil world. We must put on Christ's righteousness for our justification, put on the Spirit and grace in Christ for sanctification, put on the Lord Jesus Christ as a garment directing you as well as to save you. How to walk: let us walk to please Him, walk honestly and in the Truth; avoiding the works of the flesh. Where there is drunkenness, usually perversions and dishonesty follow.

Our walk should not be with strife and cruel words. We assume the place of God when we act upon our own judgments of others; those who partake of certain things that may offend our thinking, who might be out of our little group. It is necessary only that the word of God certifies their actions and not us. We all are likely to make our own views of the truth, considering things lawful, which to others may appear rebellious. Accordingly, believers often condemn each other of matters of little or no significance to God.

Self-seekers

No one should be a self-seeker. The business of our lives is not to please ourselves, or others, but to please God. True grace makes Christ complete in us! Although we are of different strengths, capacities, and practice, we are the Lords. Christ is both Lords of the living, to rule them, and of the dead, to revive them, and raise them up.

We should not be swift to judge or despise one another, because we all must give an account of our works compared to the Gospel. Therefore, every man should search his own heart and life. We must be watchful of saying or doing things, which may cause others to stumble or fall.

Even though we are subject to fail, Christ deals gently with those who do. Christ denied Himself, and died for the Church, so we also should are to keep from any immoderation. We can't keep others from speaking evil, but we mustn't give them any occasion to speak evil of us. Even though there may be some things that are lawful for us, we must deny ourselves in many areas so that we may not hurt our good witness. If you value your reputation of the good that you profess; let's not cause others to speak evil of us. Righteousness, peace, and joy, are words that should mean a considerable deal and should be our most concern in appearing before Him justified, and sanctified by the Spirit of his grace.

Those that don't seek for peace are sometimes the ones who cry the loudest for it. Meekness, humility, self-denial, and love, make way for great peace, but if we quarrel and fight among ourselves, we cannot teach another when the need arises. Many in the early church quarreled over certain foods; meat and drink; nothing destroys our blessings more than fulfilling fleshly lusts.

There are some, who apply lawful things in an unlawfully manner. This involves many different things, whereby a brother or sister may be deceived and led away into sin. We are warned by Paul to enjoy the freedom in our liberties of grace, but don't allow others to become offended by our wrong use of them.

How excellent are the blessings of Christ's kingdom, which do not consist in any outward rites or ceremonies? His righteousness, His peace, and His joy, all are within the Holy Spirit! We sometimes think of dying to Christ as a martyr's death, but death is only the separation from one place to another. Our dying is to the flesh, separating ourselves from our sin nature, and living unto our new nature in Christ.

Do Unto Others Life-style

We are not to please others, to our benefit, but theirs. We are not to follow their wickedness, or humor or please their sinful ways. We know that the way of the ungodly will always conflict with the wisdom of God.

Christ's lived the ultimate self-denying, do unto other's lifestyle, not considering for one moment, His spotless purity and holiness. Nothing could have been more agonizing, than to be made the sin for an ungrateful world, then your own heavenly Father turns away in your darkest hour of need.

Our every act should prove of our union in Christ and how beneficial the Gospel of grace shows forth in our lives! When focused upon the power of the Holy Spirit, what wonderful effects it produces! Let us, as God's righteous people not give in to any fleshly seeds of doubt.

Although Christ knows what we need to fulfill our life here on earth, we are still required to ask in faith, trusting in His words. Don't be double-minded for, that person should expect nothing from the Lord" (*James 1:6*). All our joy in receiving answers to our prayers depends upon "praying Gods will" so, let's be serious when we pray that Christ's blessing of grace may come upon all believers. Praying His word is not praying our religious thoughts! If Jesus gave us a promise, "pray (say) that promise," not your present circumstance! If you want sincerely to pray the perfect will of God, pray according to one Corinthians, Chapter 14, verse 2, "For the person who speaks in an unknown tongue does not speak to people but to God. Indeed, no one understands him, because he is speaking secrets in the Spirit" Emphasis added).

Many may name Christ as their Lord, but are far from serving him. By following their personal sensual interests, they corrupt the gospel and pervert their individual judgments. We are to be watchful, "keeping our minds" with all diligence, for it is the common policy of deceivers to set their sights upon those who are insecure in the knowledge of God.

We are directed to be wise and not to be deceived by false teachings! So simple are these words, but so true. The main favor of grace that we should expect from God is our victory over Satan's devices. These include every design and tactic against our will and emotions, which seek to kill, steal, and destroy. Satan's tactics are to keep us from the peace of God; this is his eternal quest. When Satan tries to prevail, don't throw your confidence away, and when you feel like giving up, activate His faith within you. Meditate on His word, speak His favors and the peace of God will intervene in your behalf, bringing with it a blissful rest.

Remember, we are called to the "obedience of faith," not the obedience of good works! We must proclaim His righteousness, His wisdom as our wisdom, His holiness as our holiness, and His faith as our faith! We are complete in Him; His peace is our peace; His fullness is our fullness. We are to give Him glory and rest within His legacy. We have an adopted birthright; the grace of our Lord Jesus Christ is with us forever. He is the Mediator of all our prayers for all eternity.

Blessed and Highly Favored

Because you have responded to the voice of your God, sought first and accepted His "kingdom of righteousness" through His Son, Jesus the Christ, goodness and mercy will follow you. This doesn't mean they are stalking you, never to give assistance, but always with you in your time of need. His legacy has come unto you and His kingdom lives within you; you are blessed and highly favored!

This undeserved favor is only available within the law of faith. Your household will see the salvation of the Lord! Your property, your work-place, your food Pantry, all is favored. Your bank account, along with every journey is also highly favored. His grace is eternal sufficient; you have the right to be the lender, not the borrower. His grace will place you in an office of authority, invariably to excel, never be behind. All because you obediently listened and accepted His call.

His grace makes you complete in Him. He has already given you all things that pertain to life and godliness. Many will see you living in His graces and hold you in respect.

The LORD will bless you and constantly keep you; His favor will regularly shine upon you and be gracious about you; He will exalt you and give you peaceful rest; His Name is upon you, and in you. His grace is with you and in you. Amen…SO LET IT BE! If you agree, then decree, go and live your destiny, live out His "Legacy of Grace."

Kingdommotivations.com
Foe speaking engagements contact:
garypippins@yahoo.com

www.ingramcontent.com/pod-product-compliance
Lightning Source LLC
Chambersburg PA
CBHW071520040426
42444CB00008B/1727